400+ Cool & Unbelievable Spacecraft Facts for Kids

Contents

Introduction	3
Chapter 1: First Space Animals	5
Chapter 2: Space Toilets	10
Chapter 3: Fastest Spacecraft	15
Chapter 4: Space Food Prep	20
Chapter 5: Largest Spacecraft Ever	25
Chapter 6: Star Navigation	30
Chapter 7: Farthest Space Travel	35
Chapter 8: Solar-Powered Spacecraft	40
Chapter 9: Space Exercise	45
Chapter 10: Tiniest Space Explorers	50
Chapter 11: Planetary Landing Missions	55
Chapter 12: Spacecraft-Earth Communication	60
Chapter 13: Longest-Running Space Missions	65
Chapter 14: Sun-Studying Spacecraft	70
Chapter 15: Space Radiation Protection	75
Chapter 16: Costliest Space Projects	80
Chapter 17: Beyond Solar System Explorers	85
Chapter 18: Spacecraft Power Generation	90
Chapter 19: First Planetary Orbiters	95
Chapter 20: Comet and Asteroid Chasers	100
Chapter 21: Extreme Temperature Survival	105
Chapter 22: Heaviest Space Cargo	110
Chapter 23: Spacecraft Formations	115
Chapter 24: Planetary Landing Techniques	120
Conclusion	125

Introduction

Hey there, space explorers! Are you ready for an out-of-this-world adventure? Buckle up, because we're about to blast off into the amazing universe of spacecraft! From the tiniest space probes to massive rockets, from the first animals in space to the coolest technology of the future, we're going to discover it all!

Imagine riding in a spacecraft that can change shape like magic, or sailing through the stars on a light beam. Picture yourself using a space toilet in zero gravity, or helping a brave little robot land on Mars. How about visiting a comet, or flying past the rings of Saturn?

In this cosmic journey, we'll meet space dogs and astronaut cats, see how spacecraft survive the scorching heat of the Sun and the freezing cold of deep space, and learn how scientists talk to robots billions of miles away. We'll explore how spacecraft work together like a team of space detectives, and discover the heaviest things ever launched into orbit (spoiler: it's as heavy as a bunch of elephants!).

From the fastest spacecraft zooming through our solar system to the clever ways astronauts exercise in space, every page is packed with awesome facts and cool stories. We'll travel to the Moon, Mars, and mysterious moons around Jupiter and Saturn. We'll even peek at future spacecraft that might one day take us to other stars!

So, are you curious about how astronauts eat in space? Want to know how we protect spacecraft from dangerous space radiation? Or maybe you're wondering how we land delicate robots on distant planets without breaking them? Well, you're in the right place!

Get ready to have your mind blown by the incredible world of spacecraft. Whether you dream of being an astronaut, an engineer, or just love learning about space, this book is your ticket to the stars. Let's start our mission to explore the final frontier – space awaits!

Chapter 1: First Space Animals

1. Meet Laika, the brave space dog! In 1957, this Russian stray became the first animal to orbit Earth. Laika rode in Sputnik 2, a small spacecraft. Though she didn't survive the journey, Laika paved the way for human space travel and is remembered as a hero.

2. Ham the Astrochimp made history in 1961. NASA sent him on a short space flight to test if animals could survive in space. Ham did great! He pushed buttons and pulled levers just like he was trained. His success showed that humans could safely travel to space too.

3. In 1963, a cat named Félicette became the first feline in space. France launched her in a rocket that flew for 15 minutes. Félicette returned safely and even got a special "kitty space suit" for her mission. She proved cats could handle space travel too!

4. Belka and Strelka were two dogs who orbited Earth in 1960. They spent a whole day in space and came back safely! Strelka later had puppies, and one was given to U.S. President Kennedy as a gift. These space pups helped scientists learn about long space flights.

5. Albert II, a brave rhesus monkey, became the first primate in space in 1949. He flew in a special rocket called a V-2. Although Albert II didn't survive the landing, his journey taught scientists important lessons about space travel and paved the way for future missions.

6. In 1968, the Soviet Union sent two tortoises to the Moon! These slow-moving explorers circled the Moon and came back to Earth. They lost some weight but were otherwise fine. These cosmic chelonians showed that even reptiles could handle space travel.

7. Fruit flies were the first animals to reach space in 1947. They flew on a V-2 rocket to see how space radiation affected living things. The flies returned safely and showed that animals could survive in space. These tiny pioneers opened the door for future space explorers.

8. In 1959, a squirrel monkey named Miss Baker flew to space with a rhesus monkey named Able. They both returned safely, making them the first primates to survive space flight. Miss Baker lived to be 27 years old and received fan mail for years after her adventure!

9. Rabbits joined the space race in 1959 when the Soviet Union sent one up with two dogs. The bunny, along with its canine crewmates, orbited Earth and returned safely. This fluffy astronaut helped scientists understand how different animals react to space conditions.

10. Mummichog fish made a splash in space history in 1973. NASA sent them to Skylab, America's first space station. These little swimmers helped scientists study how fish behave in zero gravity. They proved that fish could adapt to life without "up" or "down"!

11. In 1985, two garden spiders named Arabella and Anita spun webs in space. They were part of a student experiment on Skylab. At first, their webs were messy, but they quickly adapted to zero gravity. These eight-legged astronauts showed how animals can adjust to new environments.

12. Nefertiti the "Spidernaut" flew to the International Space Station in 2012. This jumping spider spent 100 days in space, catching prey in zero gravity. Nefertiti returned to Earth and lived at the Smithsonian Museum, where visitors could see this amazing space explorer.

13. Mice first ventured into space in 1950. Scientists sent them up in rockets to study the effects of cosmic radiation. These tiny astronauts helped pave the way for human space exploration by showing how living creatures react to the space environment.

14. In 1968, the Apollo 7 mission carried brine shrimp eggs to space. The eggs hatched in orbit, becoming the first animals born in space. This experiment helped scientists understand how space affects animal development and reproduction.

15. Newts became space pioneers in 1985. The Soviet Union sent them to study how microgravity affects limb regeneration. These amphibian astronauts regrew amputated limbs in space, helping scientists learn about healing in zero gravity.

16. Jellyfish took a space journey in 1991 aboard Space Shuttle Columbia. Scientists wanted to see how these creatures, which rely on gravity to know up from down, would develop in space. The space jellyfish had trouble adjusting when they returned to Earth.

17. In 2007, tardigrades became the first animals to survive exposure to open space. These tiny "water bears" were exposed to the vacuum and radiation of space for 10 days. They returned to Earth alive, proving they're one of the toughest creatures in the universe!

18. Quail eggs hatched aboard the Russian space station Mir in 1990. The chicks had trouble standing up in zero gravity but eventually learned to "swim" through the air. This experiment helped scientists understand how animals adapt to being born in space.

19. Geckos made headlines in 2014 when Russia sent them to space to study animal mating in zero gravity. These lizards spent 44 days orbiting Earth. Their mission helped scientists learn about how space affects animal reproduction.

20. In 2018, a colony of ants flew to the International Space Station. Scientists watched how they built their nests and worked together in zero gravity. These space ants showed that even tiny insects can adapt to life off Earth!

Chapter 2: Space Toilets

1. Astronauts can't just flush in space! They use special toilets with suction. When an astronaut needs to go, they sit on a small seat and turn on a fan. The fan creates suction that pulls everything into a container. It's like a vacuum cleaner for poop!

2. Peeing in space is tricky! Astronauts use a funnel attached to a hose. The funnel comes in different sizes for boys and girls. When they pee, a fan sucks the liquid away. The pee is then recycled into clean drinking water. Astronauts say it tastes better than tap water!

3. What happens to space poop? It gets stored in special containers. When these are full, they're put into a cargo ship. This ship then leaves the space station and burns up in Earth's atmosphere. So, space poop becomes a shooting star!

4. Astronaut diapers are real! Called Maximum Absorbency Garments (MAGs), they're used during launches, landings, and spacewalks. These super-absorbent underpants can hold up to a liter of liquid. They keep astronauts comfy when they can't reach the space toilet.

5. Using the space toilet takes practice! Before going to space, astronauts train with a toilet simulator. It has a camera in the bowl so they can see if they're positioned correctly. They practice until they can use it perfectly every time.

6. Space toilets cost a lot! The toilet on the International Space Station cost $19 million. That's because it needs to work perfectly in zero gravity and last for years without repairs. It's probably the most expensive toilet in the universe!

7. Toilet paper in space is just like on Earth, but astronauts have to be careful not to let it float away! They secure it with Velcro and use it sparingly. Every bit of weight counts on a spacecraft, so they can't bring too much.

8. In the early days of space travel, astronauts used plastic bags for poop. They had to knead the bag to mix in a special germ-killing liquid. It wasn't very fun, but it worked! Luckily, we've come a long way since then with much better space toilets.

9. Space toilets have toe bars! Astronauts hook their feet under these bars to stay in place while using the toilet. Without gravity to hold them down, they might float away mid-poop! The toe bars help them stay put and do their business.

10. What if the space toilet breaks? Astronauts have emergency backup systems. One is called the Apollo Bag, named after the Apollo missions. It's basically a sticky plastic bag that attaches directly to their bottom. Not comfortable, but better than nothing!

11. Astronauts can't use regular soap to wash their hands after using the space toilet. Instead, they use wet wipes and hand sanitizer. The wet wipes are secured so they don't float away. Keeping clean is super important in the closed environment of a spacecraft.

12. Space toilets have different settings for number one and number two. For pee, the toilet uses a gentle suction. For poop, it uses stronger suction and even has a special fan to control odors. It's like a smart toilet in space!

13. The first woman in space, Valentina Tereshkova, had to use a special device because the spacecraft wasn't designed for women. It was basically a tube with a rubber seal. Since then, space agencies have made sure toilets work well for everyone.

14. On the Moon, astronauts didn't have a toilet in their spacesuits. Instead, they wore special underwear with built-in collectors. When they got back to the spacecraft, they had to seal these in special bags. Space travel can be messy!

15. The Space Shuttle had a toilet that used airflow to move waste. It was so powerful it could suck up small objects if they got too close! Astronauts had to be careful not to lose small items near the toilet.

16. In space, astronauts can't just flush and forget. They have to clean the toilet after each use. They use disinfectant wipes to clean the seat and funnel. Keeping the space toilet clean is an important part of an astronaut's daily routine.

17. The International Space Station has two toilets for up to seven astronauts. That's not many! Astronauts sometimes have to wait in line to use the bathroom, just like at school. But at least their wait is in zero gravity!

18. Space poop doesn't just disappear. Scientists study it! They analyze astronaut waste to learn about how space affects the human body. It's a stinky job, but it helps keep astronauts healthy on long space missions.

19. The newest space toilet, launched in 2020, is smaller, lighter, and works better for women. It even has a special tube for menstruation. Space agencies are always trying to improve space toilets to make life in space more comfortable.

20. What about space barf? Astronauts sometimes get sick in space, so they have special barf bags. These bags have a lining that traps the mess inside, even in zero gravity. Astronauts call it the "emesis containment system" - a fancy name for a puke bag!

Chapter 3: Fastest Spacecraft

1. Meet Parker Solar Probe, the speediest spacecraft ever! It zooms around the Sun at a mind-blowing 430,000 miles per hour. That's fast enough to fly from New York to Tokyo in less than a minute! This super-quick probe is helping us learn about the Sun's outer corona.

2. Helios 2 was a real speed demon! Launched in 1976, it held the speed record for over 40 years. This solar probe raced around the Sun at 157,000 miles per hour. That's like circling Earth seven times in just one hour!

3. New Horizons, the spacecraft that visited Pluto, is super speedy too. It left Earth faster than any spacecraft before it, zooming away at 36,000 miles per hour. That's about 50 times faster than a jet plane! New Horizons is now exploring beyond our solar system.

4. Juno, Jupiter's speedy visitor, broke records when it entered the giant planet's orbit. It reached a top speed of 165,000 miles per hour relative to Earth. That's fast enough to zip around our planet's equator in just nine minutes!

5. Voyager 1, launched in 1977, is the fastest human-made object to leave our solar system. It's still speeding away at 38,000 miles per hour. Even at that speed, it took 35 years to reach interstellar space! Voyager 1 carries a golden record with sounds from Earth.

6. The Galileo probe set a speed record when it plunged into Jupiter's atmosphere. It reached a whopping 108,000 miles per hour before burning up. That's 50 times faster than a speeding bullet! Galileo's sacrifice taught us a lot about Jupiter's composition.

7. Stardust, a comet-chasing spacecraft, became the fastest returning object to Earth. It hit our atmosphere at 28,900 miles per hour in 2006. That's 10 times faster than a bullet! Its special heat shield protected it during this blazing reentry.

8. Solar Probe Plus, planned for the future, might become the new speed champ. Scientists think it could reach speeds up to 450,000 miles per hour as it swoops near the Sun. That's fast enough to get from Earth to the Moon in just 30 minutes!

9. The Cassini spacecraft reached incredible speeds during its "Grand Finale" dive into Saturn. It hit about 75,000 miles per hour before disintegrating in Saturn's atmosphere. Cassini's fast finish ended its amazing 20-year mission exploring Saturn and its moons.

10. MESSENGER, the first spacecraft to orbit Mercury, had to be speedy to catch the swift planet. It reached 150,000 miles per hour during its final approach. That's like traveling from New York to Los Angeles in just one minute!

11. The twin STEREO spacecraft, which study the Sun, reached a combined speed of 18,000 miles per hour during launch. That's the fastest speed ever achieved by two spacecraft launched together. They now orbit the Sun, giving us a 3D view of solar storms.

12. BepiColombo, on its way to Mercury, will reach speeds up to 155,000 miles per hour. It uses the gravity of Earth, Venus, and Mercury to speed up. This cosmic "slingshot" effect helps BepiColombo save fuel while reaching amazing speeds.

13. The Ulysses probe, which studied the Sun's poles, reached 200,000 miles per hour during its mission. It used Jupiter's gravity to fling itself out of the ecliptic plane. Ulysses' speed helped it become the first spacecraft to fly over the Sun's poles.

14. Genesis, a solar wind sample return mission, re-entered Earth's atmosphere at 24,700 miles per hour. That's fast enough to fly around the entire Earth in just one hour! Unfortunately, its parachute failed, but scientists still recovered valuable solar particles.

15. The Mariner 10 probe reached 135,000 miles per hour on its way to Mercury. It was the first spacecraft to use a gravity assist maneuver, borrowing speed from Venus to reach Mercury. This clever trick is now used by many speedy spacecraft.

16. OSIRIS-REx, an asteroid sample return mission, will enter Earth's atmosphere at 27,000 miles per hour in 2023. Its heat shield will protect the precious asteroid samples during this blazing fast reentry. Scientists can't wait to study these space rocks!

17. The Hayabusa2 spacecraft returned asteroid samples to Earth at a speedy 26,640 miles per hour. Its capsule used Earth's atmosphere like a brake, slowing down just enough for a safe landing. The samples it brought back are helping us understand asteroid formation.

18. The Deep Impact probe slammed into comet Tempel 1 at 23,000 miles per hour. That's like flying from New York to Los Angeles in just 7 minutes! This high-speed collision helped scientists learn what's inside a comet.

19. The Rosetta spacecraft's Philae lander touched down on a comet at walking speed - just 2 miles per hour. But Rosetta itself zoomed around the Sun at up to 84,000 miles per hour during its mission. Sometimes, spacecraft need to be both fast and slow!

20. Future spacecraft might use light sails to reach incredible speeds. These thin, mirror-like sails would be pushed by sunlight or lasers. Scientists think they could reach up to 20% of the speed of light - that's 134 million miles per hour!

Chapter 4: Space Food Prep

1. Astronauts can't use regular salt and pepper in space. The tiny grains would float away and clog air vents or get in astronauts' eyes! Instead, they use liquid salt and pepper. These special liquids stick to the food, making meals tasty without making a mess.

2. Ever heard of a tortilla launcher? In space, astronauts use a special gadget to warm up tortillas. It looks like a small plastic tube. They put a tortilla inside, close the lid, and wait. Soon, a warm tortilla pops out, ready for space tacos!

3. Astronauts love ice cream, but regular ice cream would make a floating mess. So, they eat freeze-dried ice cream instead. It looks like a crunchy block and doesn't need to be kept cold. When astronauts eat it, it melts in their mouth just like real ice cream!

4. Space food often comes in pouches. Astronauts add hot or cold water to rehydrate their meals. They use a special needle-like tool to inject water into the pouch. After a few minutes of shaking, their floating feast is ready to eat!

5. Bread is banned in space! Crumbs can float around and damage equipment. Instead, astronauts eat tortillas. They're flat, flexible, and don't make crumbs. Astronauts use them for everything from sandwiches to pizza bases. Space tacos are a favorite meal!

6. Astronauts have a special drink bag for space beverages. It looks like a juice pouch with a straw, but the straw has a clamp to stop the liquid from floating out. When they're done, they can roll up the empty bag to save space. No spills in zero gravity!

7. In space, opening a fizzy drink would be a disaster! The bubbles wouldn't rise to the top, so the whole drink would explode out of the can. Instead, astronauts drink special flat versions of their favorite sodas. No bubbles means no mess!

8. Astronauts can't use normal forks and knives in space. Food would float off! They use special utensils with bent handles that help food stick. Some even have magnets to stick to their trays. With these tools, astronauts can eat without their dinner flying away!

9. Space food needs to last a long time without refrigeration. Scientists use special ways to preserve it, like freeze-drying or thermostabilization. These big words mean removing water or heating food to kill germs. This keeps space food fresh for months or even years!

10. Astronauts can grow their own salad in space! They use special plant growth chambers with LED lights. These space gardens provide fresh lettuce, which is a tasty treat after months of packaged food. Imagine eating a salad that was grown while orbiting Earth!

11. In the early days of space travel, astronauts ate puréed food from tubes, like toothpaste! It wasn't very tasty, but it was easy to eat in zero gravity. Today's astronauts have much yummier options, including many foods that look and taste like what we eat on Earth.

12. Space food packaging is really important. It needs to be light, easy to open, and keep food fresh for a long time. Scientists are always trying to make it better. Some new packages can even heat up food without electricity, using a special chemical reaction!

13. Astronauts can't have open flames in space, so there's no grilling or frying. Instead, they have a special space oven that uses heat and fans to warm food. It's not as fast as a microwave, but it gets the job done. Warm space lasagna, anyone?

14. Making coffee in space is tricky without gravity. Astronauts use special coffee pouches with a one-way valve. They add hot water through the valve, then shake the pouch to mix. The valve lets them sip their coffee without it floating away. Space lattes, anyone?

15. Astronauts need extra calcium in space because zero gravity can weaken bones. So, space nutritionists add extra calcium to their food. They might have orange juice with added calcium for breakfast or calcium-enriched chocolate pudding for dessert. Yum and healthy!

16. In space, you can't just sprinkle spices on your food - they'd float away! So, astronauts use liquid spices. These come in small bottles, like eye drops. A few drops of liquid garlic or liquid soy sauce can make space food much tastier!

17. Astronauts have to be careful not to make crumbs in space. Floating crumbs could get into important equipment. So, many space foods are designed to be bite-sized or sticky. Things like nuts are coated in gelatin to keep them from breaking into small pieces.

18. Space food isn't just about taste - it's also about nutrition. Astronauts need the right balance of vitamins and minerals to stay healthy in space. Nutritionists carefully plan each meal to make sure astronauts get everything they need, even on long missions.

19. Some astronauts like spicy food in space because their sense of taste changes. The lack of gravity makes fluids shift in their bodies, giving them stuffy noses. Spicy foods help them taste their meals better. Hot sauce is a popular item on space missions!

20. Astronauts can't keep leftovers in space. There's no refrigerator, and old food could grow dangerous bacteria. So, they have to eat all their food or throw away what's left. This means careful planning to make sure no food is wasted on the space station.

Chapter 5: Largest Spacecraft Ever

1. The International Space Station (ISS) is the largest spacecraft ever built! It's as big as a football field and weighs as much as 450 cars. Astronauts from different countries live and work there, orbiting Earth every 90 minutes. It's like a giant floating science lab in space!

2. China's Tiangong Space Station is growing bigger! It's not as large as the ISS yet, but it's still huge. When complete, it will be about the size of a five-bedroom house. Chinese astronauts, called taikonauts, will live there and do experiments in space.

3. The Space Shuttle was once the largest reusable spacecraft. It was as big as a jumbo jet! The shuttle could carry seven astronauts and lots of cargo. It looked like a plane but flew to space like a rocket. Sadly, we don't use them anymore, but they were amazing!

4. The Saturn V rocket was the tallest and heaviest spacecraft ever launched. It stood taller than the Statue of Liberty! This giant rocket took astronauts to the Moon during the Apollo missions. It was so powerful it could launch 130 tons into orbit - that's like 40 elephants!

5. The Mir Space Station was Russia's floating home in space for 15 years. It was about the size of six school buses put together. Mir means "peace" in Russian. It was the largest spacecraft in orbit until the ISS took its place.

6. The Skylab was America's first space station. It was as big as a three-bedroom house and orbited Earth for six years. Astronauts lived there for months at a time, studying the Sun and how the human body changes in space. It was like a holiday home in orbit!

7. The Hubble Space Telescope is the size of a large school bus. It's not a home for astronauts, but it's one of the largest observatory spacecraft. Hubble orbits high above Earth's atmosphere, taking amazing pictures of distant stars and galaxies.

8. The James Webb Space Telescope is the largest space telescope ever built. Its main mirror is as big as a tennis court! It had to be folded up like origami to fit in the rocket. Now it's far out in space, showing us the universe like we've never seen before.

9. The Lunar Gateway will be a small space station orbiting the Moon. It won't be as big as the ISS, but it will be the largest spacecraft around the Moon. Astronauts will use it as a pit stop on their way to explore the lunar surface.

10. The Orion spacecraft is NASA's newest vehicle for sending astronauts into deep space. It's about the size of two minivans and can carry four astronauts. Orion is tough enough to travel to the Moon and maybe even Mars one day!

11. The Tiangong-1 was China's first space station. It was about the size of a school bus and orbited Earth for nearly 7 years. Although it was smaller than other space stations, it was a big step for China's space program.

12. The Dream Chaser is a new spacecraft that looks like a mini space shuttle. It's about the size of a small private jet. This cool craft will carry cargo to the ISS and land on a runway like an airplane when it returns to Earth.

13. The Bigelow Expandable Activity Module (BEAM) is like a balloon for space! It's attached to the ISS and can inflate to the size of a small bedroom. This technology could help build even larger spacecraft in the future.

14. The SpaceX Starship is set to be the largest and most powerful rocket ever built. When finished, it will be taller than a 30-story building! This giant spacecraft is designed to carry people to the Moon, Mars, and beyond.

15. The Soviet Buran was a spacecraft as big as the American Space Shuttle. It only flew to space once, without any crew. Although it's not used anymore, it showed that large, reusable spacecraft could be built by different countries.

16. The X-37B is a secret space plane that can stay in orbit for years at a time. It's about the size of a small school bus. Nobody knows exactly what it does up there, but it's one of the largest unmanned spacecraft currently in use.

17. The Salyut space stations were some of the earliest large spacecraft in orbit. There were seven of them, each about the size of a train car. They helped pave the way for bigger stations like Mir and the ISS.

18. The Shenzhou spacecraft is China's vehicle for sending taikonauts to space. It's about the size of a small RV and can carry three people. Shenzhou means "Divine Vessel" in Chinese, and it's helped China become a major space power.

19. The Artemis program will use several large spacecraft to return humans to the Moon. This includes the giant SLS rocket, which is almost as tall as the Saturn V. It will launch the Orion capsule and parts for a new lunar space station.

20. Future spacecraft might be even larger! Scientists are designing concepts for enormous ships that could carry hundreds of people to Mars or beyond. These space arks might be as big as cities, with gardens, schools, and everything needed for long journeys through space.

Chapter 6: Star Navigation

1. Long ago, sailors used stars to find their way across oceans. Spacecraft do the same thing in space! They have special cameras that take pictures of stars. Computers compare these pictures to star maps, helping the spacecraft know exactly where it is.

2. Spacecraft use a cool tool called a star tracker. It's like a high-tech telescope that can recognize star patterns. When the star tracker spots familiar constellations, it tells the spacecraft which way to go. It's like having a stellar GPS in space!

3. The North Star, Polaris, is super important for Earth navigation. But in deep space, spacecraft use many different stars. They look for bright, easy-to-spot stars all around them. This helps them figure out their position no matter which way they're facing.

4. Some spacecraft have a backup navigation system using the Sun. If they can't see enough stars, they look at the Sun's position instead. It's like using a giant space compass! This helps spacecraft stay on course even when star-gazing isn't possible.

5. Spacecraft use math to navigate by stars. They measure the angles between different stars and compare them to known star positions. This triangulation helps them calculate their exact location in space. It's like solving a giant celestial puzzle!

6. The Hubble Space Telescope uses stars to keep itself steady. It has special gyroscopes that lock onto guide stars. This helps Hubble stay perfectly still while taking pictures of distant galaxies. It's like using stellar tripods for the ultimate space camera!

7. When spacecraft are near planets, they use both stars and the planet to navigate. They might use the planet's moons or surface features along with star positions. This combination helps them make super accurate movements, like parking in a precise orbit.

8. Some spacecraft create their own star maps. They take pictures of the stars around them and build a custom map. This helps them navigate in parts of space where we don't have detailed star charts. It's like making your own space roadmap!

9. The New Horizons spacecraft, which visited Pluto, used star navigation on its long journey. It would regularly check its position against the stars. This helped it stay on course for nine years as it traveled over 3 billion miles to reach Pluto!

10. Space shuttles used to have a special window just for star navigation. Astronauts could use this window and a space sextant to measure star positions. It was a backup in case the electronic systems failed. Sometimes, old-school methods work great in high-tech situations!

11. The Voyager spacecraft, now in interstellar space, still use stars to navigate. They're so far away that radio signals from Earth take hours to reach them. Star navigation helps them stay on course in the vast emptiness between stars.

12. Star trackers on spacecraft are so precise they can detect if the spacecraft tilts by less than one degree. That's like noticing if a huge soccer field tilted by the thickness of a piece of paper! This precision helps spacecraft point their antennas exactly towards Earth.

13. Some spacecraft use pulsars, rapidly spinning neutron stars, for navigation. Pulsars send out regular radio pulses, like cosmic lighthouses. By timing these pulses, spacecraft can figure out their position. It's like having stellar GPS stations spread across the galaxy!

14. The Apollo missions to the Moon used star navigation as a backup. Astronauts had a special telescope and computer to measure star positions. This helped them check if they were on the right path to the Moon. It was like double-checking your map on a really long road trip!

15. Future spacecraft might use X-ray emissions from pulsars to navigate. This could work even when optical star trackers can't see stars. It's like having night-vision goggles for spacecraft, allowing them to navigate in any conditions!

16. The Galileo spacecraft, which explored Jupiter, used a clever trick with stars. It would spin slowly and scan the stars in a circle. This helped it stay oriented correctly as it swooped past Jupiter's moons. It's like doing a stellar pirouette to keep your bearings!

17. Some small satellites use simple star trackers made from ordinary cameras. They take pictures of stars and use smart computer programs to figure out which stars they're seeing. It's like playing a giant game of connect-the-dots with stars!

18. The James Webb Space Telescope uses very faint guide stars to stay steady. It can lock onto stars too dim for humans to see with the naked eye. This lets it point at distant galaxies with amazing accuracy. It's like using stellar laser pointers!

19. Spacecraft heading to Mars use stars to make sure they're on the right path. They regularly check their position against the stars and make tiny adjustments. This keeps them from drifting off course during the long journey. It's like using stellar stepping stones to Mars!

20. In the future, spacecraft might use artificial stars for navigation. These would be special satellites that act like beacons in space. Spacecraft could use these artificial stars along with real ones to navigate even more accurately. It's like adding extra constellations to the sky!

Chapter 7: Farthest Space Travel

1. Voyager 1 is the farthest traveling spacecraft ever! Launched in 1977, it's now over 14 billion miles from Earth. That's like circling our planet 600,000 times! It's so far away that radio signals from Earth take over 21 hours to reach it. Voyager 1 is truly our cosmic explorer!

2. Voyager 2, Voyager 1's twin, is the second farthest spacecraft. It's over 12 billion miles from Earth! Voyager 2 is the only spacecraft to visit all four giant planets: Jupiter, Saturn, Uranus, and Neptune. It's like the ultimate space road trip!

3. New Horizons, famous for visiting Pluto, is the third farthest spacecraft. It's zooming through space at 36,000 miles per hour! That's 50 times faster than a jet plane. Even at this super speed, it took 9 years to reach Pluto. Space is really, really big!

4. Pioneer 10 was the first spacecraft to reach Jupiter and is now heading out of our solar system. It's over 11 billion miles away! Pioneer 10 carries a golden plaque with a message for aliens, just in case it meets any on its cosmic journey.

5. Pioneer 11 followed its twin, Pioneer 10, into deep space. After visiting Jupiter and Saturn, it's now over 10 billion miles from Earth. That's so far that its radio signals are too weak for us to hear anymore. It's like a silent explorer in the cosmic ocean.

6. The Voyager spacecraft are so far away, they've entered interstellar space. This means they've gone beyond the bubble of particles and magnetic fields created by our Sun. They're the first human-made objects to travel between the stars!

7. If you could drive a car to where Voyager 1 is now, it would take about 20 million years! That's longer than humans have existed on Earth. It shows just how incredibly far our spacecraft have traveled.

8. The messages we send to far-off spacecraft take a long time to arrive. When scientists send a command to Voyager 1, it takes 21 hours to get there. Then they have to wait another 21 hours for Voyager's reply. It's like having a very slow conversation across space!

9. Voyager 1 is so far away that from its viewpoint, Earth appears as a tiny, pale blue dot. Carl Sagan, a famous scientist, said this view reminds us how small and precious our planet is in the vast cosmic arena.

10. The Voyager spacecraft carry golden records with sounds and images from Earth. These are like time capsules of our planet. If aliens ever find them, they'll learn about Earth's life and cultures. It's our cosmic message in a bottle!

11. New Horizons is heading towards the Kuiper Belt, a region of icy objects beyond Neptune. It's already over 5 billion miles from Earth and still going! Scientists hope it will teach us about the outer edges of our solar system.

12. The Parker Solar Probe isn't going as far as other spacecraft, but it's the fastest! It's studying the Sun up close. When it reaches its closest point to the Sun, it'll be moving at about 430,000 miles per hour. That's fast enough to get from Earth to the Moon in 30 minutes!

13. Voyager 1 is so far away that it sees stars in slightly different positions than we do on Earth. This change in perspective is called parallax. It's like how things seem to move when you look out a car window, but on a much bigger scale!

14. The farthest spacecraft are now beyond the heliosphere, the region of space influenced by our Sun's solar wind. They're in true interstellar space, where the environment is shaped by other stars. It's like they've left our solar neighborhood and entered the cosmic suburbs!

15. Even though Voyager 1 and 2 are incredibly far away, they're still really close in terms of the size of our galaxy. If our galaxy were the size of the USA, the Voyagers would have only traveled about the length of a soccer field!

16. The Voyager spacecraft will be the farthest-traveling objects made by humans for a long time. In about 40,000 years, they'll pass closer to other stars than they are to our Sun. Maybe future alien archaeologists will find them and learn about Earth!

17. The next star Voyager 1 will pass by is called Gliese 445, but that won't happen for about 40,000 years. Space is so big that even at Voyager's incredible speed, it takes a very long time to reach other stars.

18. Scientists think the Voyager spacecraft will keep working until about 2025. After that, they'll be too far away to communicate with Earth. But they'll keep flying through space forever, carrying their golden records as eternal ambassadors from Earth.

19. The farthest distance traveled by a spacecraft with people on board was set by the Apollo 13 astronauts. They looped around the far side of the Moon, reaching a distance of 248,655 miles from Earth. That's the farthest humans have ever been from home!

20. Future spacecraft might go even farther than Voyager 1. Scientists are designing special engines that could take spacecraft to nearby stars in just a few decades. Imagine being able to visit other solar systems! The cosmic adventure is just beginning.

Chapter 8: Solar-Powered Spacecraft

1. The Juno spacecraft orbiting Jupiter is like a giant solar-powered pinwheel! Its three huge solar panels stretch out 66 feet, longer than a school bus. These panels soak up sunlight to power Juno as it studies the biggest planet in our solar system.

2. IKAROS, a Japanese spacecraft, was the first to use a solar sail in deep space. Imagine a kite as big as six tennis courts, but super thin like plastic wrap. Sunlight pushes on this sail, moving the spacecraft through space without any fuel!

3. NASA's Dawn spacecraft used ion engines powered by the sun to visit two different asteroids. It's like a super-efficient space car that never runs out of gas! Dawn's solar panels turned sunlight into electricity, which then pushed out ions to move the spacecraft.

4. The Solar Orbiter is a spacecraft that gets really close to the Sun. Its solar panels are special - they can withstand temperatures hot enough to melt lead! This tough little spacecraft uses the Sun's energy to power its instruments while studying our nearest star.

5. LightSail 2 is a tiny spacecraft about the size of a loaf of bread, but its solar sail is as big as a boxing ring! It orbits Earth, powered only by sunlight pushing on its sail. It's proving that even small spacecraft can use the Sun's power to move through space.

6. The Parker Solar Probe gets closer to the Sun than any spacecraft before it. Its solar panels are super smart - they hide behind a special shield when it gets too hot, then pop out to catch some rays when it's safe. It's like a spacecraft playing peek-a-boo with the Sun!

7. Mars Cube One, or MarCO, were two tiny solar-powered spacecraft that went to Mars. Each one was only as big as a cereal box! They used the Sun's energy to power their radios, helping relay messages from the InSight lander back to Earth. Tiny but mighty!

8. The Planetary Society's LightSail program is testing solar sails for future space exploration. These sails are so thin, you could fit one in your backpack! But when unfolded in space, they're as big as a classroom. Sunlight bouncing off the sail pushes it through space.

9. The Rosetta spacecraft traveled for 10 years to reach a comet, all powered by the Sun. Its huge solar panels could power two households! Even far from the Sun, where sunlight is weak, Rosetta had enough power to study its comet and send pictures back to Earth.

10. BepiColombo, a spacecraft on its way to Mercury, has a special trick. It uses both the Sun's light and heat to make power! Its solar panels catch sunlight, and its antennas collect heat. This helps it stay powered up even when it's close to the hot planet Mercury.

11. The International Space Station has solar panels as long as a football field! These giant panels turn to face the Sun as the station orbits Earth, providing power for astronauts to live and work in space. It's like a huge solar-powered house floating above our planet.

12. OSIRIS-REx, the spacecraft that collected samples from an asteroid, uses solar power for its journey. Its panels can rotate like a shoulder to always face the Sun. This helps it stay powered up even when it's moving around the asteroid to find the best place to grab a sample.

13. Solar-powered CubeSats are tiny spacecraft about the size of a tissue box. They're covered in small solar panels that power their instruments and radios. These little explorers are cheap to launch, so students and small companies can send experiments to space!

14. The Lucy spacecraft is on a mission to visit Jupiter's Trojan asteroids. It has huge solar panels that open up like a fan. These panels will power Lucy on its 12-year journey, making it the farthest-traveling solar-powered spacecraft ever!

15. The Mars Helicopter, Ingenuity, uses solar power to fly on another planet! Its small solar panel charges its batteries during the Martian day. Then it uses that stored energy to spin its rotors and fly in Mars' thin atmosphere. It's like a cosmic drone!

16. The Solar Cruiser, a future NASA mission, will have the largest solar sail ever - about the size of a baseball diamond! This gigantic sail will use sunlight to propel the spacecraft, potentially allowing it to hover over one spot on the Sun. It's like a solar-powered UFO!

17. The NEA Scout is a tiny spacecraft that will use a solar sail to visit a near-Earth asteroid. Its sail is as big as a school bus but thinner than a human hair! This little explorer will use the Sun's push to navigate to its target asteroid.

18. The JUICE spacecraft, heading to Jupiter's moons, has solar panels covering an area larger than a basketball court. These huge panels will help it stay powered even in the dim sunlight near Jupiter. It's like having a solar-powered flashlight that works even in the dark!

19. Psyche, a future NASA mission to a metal asteroid, will use solar-electric propulsion. It's like a space tugboat powered by the Sun! The spacecraft will use solar energy to create electric fields that push out ions, slowly but steadily moving it through space.

20. The Deep Space Gateway, a planned space station near the Moon, will use solar electric propulsion to maintain its orbit. Its giant solar arrays will power ion engines, allowing it to move around lunar orbit without using much fuel. It's like a solar-powered Moon ferry!

Chapter 9: Space Exercise

1. In space, astronauts float around because there's no gravity. This might sound fun, but it can make their muscles and bones weak. To stay healthy, they exercise for about two hours every day. It's like having PE class in space!

2. The treadmill on the space station is special. Astronauts wear a harness that's attached to bungee cords. These cords pull them down towards the treadmill so they can run. Without this, they'd float away! It's like running while wearing a super bouncy backpack.

3. Astronauts use a bicycle that doesn't go anywhere! It's called a cycle ergometer. They strap their feet in and pedal, but the bike stays in one spot. This helps keep their leg muscles strong. Imagine riding a bike that's stuck in place but still gives you a workout!

4. The space station has a special machine called ARED (Advanced Resistive Exercise Device). It uses vacuum cylinders to create resistance, like lifting weights on Earth. Astronauts can do squats, deadlifts, and bench presses. It's like a whole gym in one machine!

5. Astronauts play catch with medicine balls in space. But instead of throwing them, they push them back and forth. This helps strengthen their arms and core muscles. It's like playing catch in a giant bubble where you're always floating!

6. Yoga in space is tricky but fun! Astronauts use straps to hold onto handrails while doing poses. This helps them stretch and stay flexible. Imagine doing a headstand while floating upside down - that's space yoga!

7. To exercise their arms, astronauts use resistance bands. They attach these elastic bands to the walls and pull on them. It's like having a bunch of giant rubber bands to play with, but it's actually a serious workout!

8. The space treadmill has a cool name - T2. Astronauts can run up to 8 miles per hour on it. That's pretty fast, especially when you're floating! They watch movies or Earth views while running to make it more fun.

9. Astronauts wear special shorts called the Pingvin suit. It has bungee cords that make it harder to move, like walking through thick mud. This helps keep their leg muscles strong even when they're not exercising. It's like wearing workout clothes all day!

10. In space, sweat doesn't drip - it forms little bubbles that float around! Astronauts use towels to wipe off these sweat bubbles during exercise. They have to be careful not to let the sweat bubbles float into equipment. It's like dodging tiny water balloons while working out!

11. Astronauts use a vibration plate to exercise their bones. They stand on a platform that shakes really fast. This tells their bones to stay strong. It's like giving your skeleton a wake-up call every day!

12. The Japanese space module has a special machine called a flywheel. Astronauts spin it with their arms, like turning a big wheel. This helps keep their arm and shoulder muscles strong. It's like playing with a giant fidget spinner!

13. Astronauts play "space soccer" for fun exercise. They use their heads or feet to bounce a soft ball off the walls. There are no goals - the point is to keep moving and have fun. Imagine playing soccer while floating in all directions!

14. To exercise their fingers and hands, astronauts use squeeze balls. These are like stress balls but harder to squeeze. This helps keep their hands strong for doing experiments and repairs. It's like giving your hands a mini-workout every day!

15. Astronauts wear heart rate monitors while exercising. These show how hard their hearts are working. If they exercise too hard or not enough, the doctors on Earth let them know. It's like having a personal trainer watching from our planet!

16. The space station has virtual reality goggles for exercise. Astronauts can wear these while on the bicycle or treadmill. They might see themselves biking through a forest or running on a beach. It's like playing a video game while working out!

17. To cool down after exercise, astronauts use small fans. The fans blow air over them to evaporate their sweat. Without gravity, sweat just sits on their skin like a wet blanket. The fans help them feel fresh again after a good workout.

18. Astronauts do "wall push-ups" in space. They float to a wall, put their hands on it, and push themselves away. It works their chest and arm muscles. Imagine doing push-ups while floating - that's how astronauts do it!

19. Some astronauts like to juggle for hand-eye coordination exercise. In zero gravity, the balls float slowly, giving more time to catch them. It's like juggling in slow motion! This fun activity helps keep their reflexes sharp.

20. After exercising, astronauts clean the equipment with special wipes. Sweat can corrode metal in space, so they have to be extra careful. It's like giving the gym equipment a bath after every workout to keep it healthy and clean!

Chapter 10: Tiniest Space Explorers

1. Meet ChipSats, the tiniest spacecraft ever! They're as small as a postage stamp and as light as a paperclip. These mini-marvels can carry tiny sensors to study space. Imagine launching a whole handful of these into orbit - it's like throwing confetti into space!

2. The KickSat mission sent 100 tiny "Sprite" satellites into space. Each Sprite was smaller than a slice of bread and thinner than a credit card. They were released from a bigger satellite like space confetti! These little explorers proved that even tiny spacecraft can work in orbit.

3. PCBSats are spacecraft the size of a cracker. They're made from the same material as computer circuit boards. These mini-missions cost less than a video game to make! Scientists use them to test new space technologies without spending too much money.

4. The smallest spacecraft to land on another world was JAXA's MINERVA-II1. These hopping robots were about the size of a tennis ball. They bounced around on the asteroid Ryugu, taking pictures and measuring temperatures. Imagine a tiny space explorer playing hopscotch on an asteroid!

5. NASA's Nanosail-D2 was a spacecraft smaller than a loaf of bread. It unfolded a sail as big as a school bus in space! This tiny ship proved that even small spacecraft can use sunlight to move around in orbit. It's like a cosmic sailboat!

6. The tiniest Mars explorer was the CROCUS, part of the Mars Polar Lander mission. It was only as big as a grapefruit! Sadly, it was lost when the lander crashed. But it showed that we can design Mars explorers small enough to fit in your lunchbox!

7. PhoneSats are spacecraft built from smartphone parts. They're about the size of a coffee mug but pack a lot of power. NASA launched some to see if phone technology could work in space. It's like sending a text message from orbit!

8. The world's smallest space telescope was SPHERE-1, about the size of a soda can. It could take pictures of stars and planets from orbit. This pint-sized observatory proved that good things come in small packages, even in space!

9. ThinSats are spacecraft as thin as a pencil and as long as a ruler. Students can build these and send experiments to space. Imagine designing your own space mission that fits in your pencil case - that's what ThinSats let kids do!

10. The StarChip is a proposed spacecraft smaller than a credit card. It's part of a plan to send tiny probes to other stars. These cosmic chips would travel at a fraction of the speed of light! It's like sending a swarm of space-faring insects to explore the galaxy.

11. FemtoSats are spacecraft smaller than a sugar cube. They're so tiny, hundreds could fit in a shoe box! Scientists are working on ways to use these micro-explorers to study Earth's upper atmosphere. It's like having a fleet of dust-sized spaceships!

12. The KalamSat was the lightest satellite ever launched, weighing about as much as a large egg. It was created by an 18-year-old student in India! This shows that even young people can design spacecraft that make it to orbit.

13. PocketQubes are tiny satellites that fit in your pocket. They're 5 centimeters on each side - smaller than a Rubik's Cube! Universities use these to teach students about space engineering. It's like building a LEGO spaceship that actually goes to orbit!

14. The Sprite spacecraft, part of the Breakthrough Starshot project, could be the smallest interstellar explorers. They're designed to be as small as a postage stamp but able to travel to other star systems. Imagine sending a letter-sized spaceship to alien worlds!

15. CubeSats are like LEGO bricks for space. The smallest ones are 10 centimeters on each side - about as big as a tissue box. They can snap together to make bigger spacecraft. It's like building with space blocks to create custom missions!

16. The JAXA's IKAROS project included tiny solar sail deployment cameras called DCAM1 and DCAM2. They were small enough to fit in your hand but took amazing pictures of the spacecraft's solar sail unfurling in space. It's like having a space selfie stick!

17. The Swarm of TubeSats project aims to launch dozens of cylindrical satellites smaller than a soda can. These tiny tubes would work together to study Earth's atmosphere. Imagine a cloud of mini space explorers surrounding our planet!

18. The PODS (Payload Occupying Discarded Stages) concept turns used rocket parts into tiny spacecraft. It's like recycling in space! These small explorers could hitch a ride on bigger missions, making space exploration more eco-friendly.

19. BeakerSats are spacecraft that fit inside a laboratory beaker. Students can build these to learn about space engineering. It's like doing a science experiment that ends up in orbit! These tiny explorers show that space missions can start right in the classroom.

20. The SunCube FemtoSat is a spacecraft smaller than a ring box. It's designed to be cheap enough for anyone to launch their own space mission. Imagine saving up your allowance to send your very own tiny spacecraft into orbit!

Chapter 11: Planetary Landing Missions

1. The Mars Rover Perseverance made a spectacular landing on Mars in 2021. It used a sky crane to lower itself gently onto the Red Planet's surface. Imagine being lowered from a flying crane onto another world! Perseverance is now exploring Mars, looking for signs of ancient life.

2. Venus got a visitor in 1970 when the Soviet Venera 7 became the first spacecraft to land on another planet. It only lasted 23 minutes in the extreme heat, but it sent back valuable data. It was like dipping a toe into a very, very hot bathtub!

3. Neil Armstrong and Buzz Aldrin became the first humans to land on another world in 1969. Their lunar lander, Eagle, touched down on the Moon. As Armstrong stepped onto the surface, he said, "That's one small step for man, one giant leap for mankind."

4. The Huygens probe landed on Saturn's moon Titan in 2005. It was the first landing in the outer solar system! Huygens discovered that Titan has rivers and lakes, but they're filled with liquid methane, not water. It's like a bizarro Earth with different liquids!

5. In 2018, NASA's InSight lander touched down on Mars to study the planet's interior. It uses a special instrument to listen for "Marsquakes." Imagine putting your ear to the ground of another planet to hear its heartbeat!

6. China's Zhurong rover landed on Mars in 2021, making China the second country to successfully operate a rover on the Red Planet. Zhurong means "God of Fire" in Chinese mythology. This fiery explorer is studying Mars' geology and searching for underground ice.

7. The Soviet Union's Venera 13 landed on Venus in 1982 and survived for 127 minutes in the planet's harsh conditions. It even sent back the first color photos from Venus' surface! It was like taking a selfie in an oven.

8. NASA's Curiosity rover made a dramatic landing on Mars in 2012 using a sky crane. It's been exploring the Gale Crater ever since, climbing a mountain and discovering that Mars once had conditions suitable for life. It's like a robotic mountain climber on another world!

9. The European Space Agency's Philae lander touched down on a comet in 2014. It was the first-ever soft landing on a comet! Although Philae bounced and ended up in a shady spot, it still sent back valuable data. Imagine landing on a cosmic snowball!

10. Japan's Hayabusa2 spacecraft landed on the asteroid Ryugu in 2019. It fired a bullet into the asteroid to kick up dust, which it then collected. It's like playing marbles with a space rock, but the prize is asteroid samples!

11. The Soviet Luna 9 became the first spacecraft to achieve a soft landing on the Moon in 1966. It sent back the first close-up images of the lunar surface. These pictures helped prove that the Moon's surface was solid enough for astronauts to walk on.

12. NASA's NEAR Shoemaker spacecraft landed on the asteroid Eros in 2001. It wasn't designed to land, but engineers decided to try anyway at the end of its mission. Surprisingly, it survived and kept sending data! It's like sticking a perfect dismount in space gymnastics.

13. India's Chandrayaan-2 mission attempted to land on the Moon's south pole in 2019. Although the lander crashed, the orbiter is still studying the Moon from above. It shows that space exploration is tough, but we learn from every attempt!

14. The Phoenix Mars Lander touched down near Mars' north pole in 2008. It discovered water ice just below the surface! Imagine digging in your backyard and finding ice on Mars. Phoenix showed us that Mars might have resources for future explorers.

15. NASA's OSIRIS-REx spacecraft briefly touched down on asteroid Bennu in 2020 to collect samples. It was more of a high-five than a landing, lasting just 6 seconds! The spacecraft is now bringing those samples back to Earth for scientists to study.

16. The Soviet Venera 9 lander sent back the first-ever photo from the surface of Venus in 1975. The image showed a barren, rocky landscape. It was like peeking through a window into a very hot, alien world!

17. China's Chang'e-4 made history in 2019 by landing on the far side of the Moon - the side we never see from Earth. It's exploring this mysterious lunar landscape and even grew plants in a special container! It's like having a garden on the Moon's secret side.

18. The Mars Polar Lander attempted to touch down near Mars' south pole in 1999. Sadly, it crashed during landing. Even though it failed, it taught engineers valuable lessons about landing on Mars. Sometimes we learn the most from our mistakes, even in space exploration!

19. Japan's MINERVA-II1 rovers landed on asteroid Ryugu in 2018. These tiny robots hop across the asteroid's surface! Imagine exploring a space rock by bouncing around on it. These little hoppers are helping us learn about asteroids up close.

20. NASA's Dragonfly mission, set to launch in 2026, will land a drone on Saturn's moon Titan. This rotorcraft will fly to different locations, exploring Titan's atmosphere and surface. It's like sending a space helicopter to an alien world!

Chapter 12: Spacecraft-Earth Communication

1. Spacecraft use radio waves to talk to Earth, just like your radio at home! But these waves travel millions of miles through space. When a spacecraft sends a message, giant dish antennas on Earth catch it. It's like playing catch with invisible balls across the solar system!

2. The Deep Space Network is a group of huge antennas that listen for spacecraft messages. There are three stations around the world, so no matter how Earth turns, one can always hear from our space explorers. It's like having big ears always pointed towards space!

3. When spacecraft are very far away, their signals get super weak. So, we use really big antennas to hear them. The largest is 70 meters wide - as big as a football field! Imagine cupping your hands around your ear to hear a whisper from across the galaxy.

4. Spacecraft sometimes use lasers to communicate! The LADEE spacecraft shot a laser message to Earth from the Moon. It's like using a flashlight to send Morse code, but much faster. This could be how we talk to astronauts on Mars in the future!

5. The New Horizons spacecraft, which visited Pluto, is so far away that its messages take over 5 hours to reach Earth. That's like saying "hello" to someone and waiting until after lunch for them to hear it! Space is really, really big.

6. The Voyager spacecraft are so distant that their signals are weaker than the power of a refrigerator light bulb by the time they reach Earth. But our big antennas can still hear them! It's like listening to a whisper from the edge of our solar system.

7. Sometimes, spacecraft play telephone in space! When the Huygens probe landed on Titan, it sent its message to the Cassini spacecraft orbiting Saturn, which then relayed it to Earth. It's like passing a note through a friend in class, but across millions of miles!

8. The Mars Rovers can't always talk directly to Earth. Sometimes Mars is in the way! So they send messages to spacecraft orbiting Mars, which then send them to Earth. It's like having a space mailman to deliver messages when you can't reach someone directly.

9. Spacecraft use special codes to send their messages. This helps protect the information from getting mixed up during its long journey through space. It's like using a secret language that only the spacecraft and Earth scientists understand.

10. When a spacecraft is behind the Sun, we can't communicate with it at all. This is called solar conjunction. It's like playing hide-and-seek, where the Sun is "it" and the spacecraft is hiding! Scientists plan ahead for these quiet periods.

11. The fastest way we've sent a message in space was with quantum entanglement. Scientists on Earth instantly affected a particle on a satellite 1,200 kilometers away! It's like having magic twins - when you tickle one, the other giggles instantly, no matter how far apart they are.

12. Some spacecraft, like MAVEN orbiting Mars, can act as communication relays. They listen for messages from rovers on the surface and send them to Earth. It's like having a space post office that collects mail from Mars and sends it to us!

13. The Juno spacecraft orbiting Jupiter uses a special antenna that can send different messages on different radio frequencies at the same time. It's like being able to write, draw, and sing all at once to tell us about Jupiter!

14. When spacecraft send pictures, they break them into tiny pieces and send them one at a time. Computers on Earth put the pieces back together, like a jigsaw puzzle. Sometimes, if pieces are missing, they have to ask the spacecraft to send them again!

15. The SETI (Search for Extraterrestrial Intelligence) project uses big antennas to listen for messages from alien civilizations. So far, we haven't heard anything. But we keep listening, just in case E.T. decides to phone home!

16. Spacecraft often use a trick called "store and forward" when communicating. They record data when Earth isn't listening, then send it all at once later. It's like saving up all your stories to tell your parents at dinner instead of calling them every five minutes!

17. The Parker Solar Probe, which studies the Sun, has a special cooling system for its antenna. Without it, the antenna would melt! Imagine needing sunscreen for your phone so you could text from next to the Sun.

18. CubeSats, which are tiny satellites, often use the same kind of radios as your Wi-Fi router at home. They're small but mighty communicators! It's like using a walkie-talkie to talk to your friend, but your friend is in orbit.

19. The Lunar Reconnaissance Orbiter uses radio waves to make maps of the Moon's surface. It's like using sound to see! The spacecraft sends radio waves that bounce off the Moon and come back, telling us about mountains and craters we can't see with cameras.

20. Future Mars missions might use a "Mars Internet" to communicate. Multiple satellites around Mars would work together to send messages, like a cosmic Wi-Fi network. Imagine checking your social media from the Red Planet!

Chapter 13: Longest-Running Space Missions

1. Voyager 1 and 2 are the longest-operating spacecraft ever! Launched in 1977, they're still working after more than 45 years. That's older than most of your parents! These space explorers have gone farther than any other human-made object, sending back data from beyond our solar system.

2. The Hubble Space Telescope has been our eye in the sky since 1990. That's over 30 years of showing us amazing space pictures! Astronauts have visited Hubble five times to fix and upgrade it. It's like giving your telescope a space tune-up!

3. Mars Odyssey has been orbiting the Red Planet since 2001. That's longer than any other Mars spacecraft! It's like having a loyal friend circling Mars for over 20 years, always ready to send us new information about our neighboring planet.

4. Pioneer 10 amazed scientists by operating for over 30 years after its 1972 launch. It was the first spacecraft to visit Jupiter and kept sending signals until 2003. Imagine a space explorer that worked longer than it took you to grow up!

5. The International Space Station (ISS) has been continuously occupied since 2000. That's more than 20 years of astronauts living in space! It's like having a house floating above Earth that's always had someone home for longer than you've been alive.

6. Landsat 5 holds the Guinness World Record for the longest-operating Earth observation satellite. It worked for 29 years, from 1984 to 2013! This space camera took millions of pictures of Earth, showing us how our planet changed over almost three decades.

7. SOHO, the Solar and Heliospheric Observatory, has been studying the Sun since 1995. That's over 25 years of staring at the Sun without hurting its eyes! SOHO has seen over 4,000 comets and helps us predict space weather.

8. Mars Reconnaissance Orbiter has been circling Mars since 2006, taking super detailed pictures. It's sent back more data than all other interplanetary missions combined! Imagine having a friend who's been taking selfies of Mars for over 15 years.

9. Cassini explored Saturn for nearly 20 years before its mission ended in 2017. It showed us Saturn's rings and moons in amazing detail. Cassini worked so long, a kid born when it launched could have graduated college by the time it finished!

10. Wind, a spacecraft studying solar wind, has been working since 1994. It's been operating for almost 30 years! Wind has survived several close calls with space junk but keeps on spinning and sending data back to Earth.

11. The 2001 Mars Odyssey has been so reliable, NASA uses it to communicate with other Mars missions. It's like having a space mailman that's been delivering messages from Mars for over 20 years without taking a single day off!

12. Geotail, launched in 1992, studies Earth's magnetosphere. It's been working for over 30 years! Geotail has orbited Earth more than 30,000 times, always watching how our planet interacts with the Sun's energy.

13. NASA's Lunar Reconnaissance Orbiter has been circling the Moon since 2009. That's over 13 years of mapping our closest neighbor! It's taken so many pictures, we now have a nearly complete map of the Moon's surface.

14. STEREO-A, studying the Sun, has been operating since 2006. It's been working for over 15 years! STEREO-A gives us a unique view of the Sun, helping predict solar storms that could affect Earth.

15. Juno has been orbiting Jupiter since 2016, studying the giant planet's storms and magnetic field. It's been working for over 6 years in Jupiter's harsh environment. That's like surviving in a giant blender of radiation for longer than you've been in school!

16. New Horizons, after zooming past Pluto in 2015, is still going strong after 16 years in space. It's now exploring the Kuiper Belt, a region of icy objects beyond Neptune. Imagine a spacecraft working longer than it took to reach its main target!

17. The Mars Express orbiter has been studying the Red Planet since 2003. That's nearly 20 years of Martian exploration! It's mapped the entire surface of Mars and even found signs of water under the planet's south pole.

18. MAVEN has been orbiting Mars since 2014, studying its atmosphere. It's been working for over 8 years! MAVEN has done over 4,000 "deep dips" into Mars' upper atmosphere, showing us how the planet lost most of its air over time.

19. The Spitzer Space Telescope worked for over 16 years before retiring in 2020. This infrared telescope showed us the universe's heat, revealing things we can't see with regular light. It worked eight years longer than planned!

20. ACE (Advanced Composition Explorer) has been studying solar wind since 1997. It's been operating for over 25 years! ACE sits between Earth and the Sun, giving us an early warning system for solar storms heading our way.

Chapter 14: Sun-Studying Spacecraft

1. The Parker Solar Probe is the closest human-made object to the Sun! It zooms through the Sun's outer atmosphere, called the corona. This spacecraft is so tough, it can withstand temperatures hot enough to melt steel. It's like sending a super-strong marshmallow to roast itself!

2. Solar Orbiter takes amazing close-up pictures of the Sun. It has a special heat shield that protects it from the intense heat. The shield is so good at its job, it keeps the spacecraft cool even when it's closer to the Sun than Mercury!

3. SOHO, the Solar and Heliospheric Observatory, has been watching the Sun since 1995. It's like a tireless lifeguard, always on the lookout for solar storms that might affect Earth. SOHO has also become great at spotting comets — it's seen over 4,000 of them!

4. The STEREO spacecraft are like twins keeping an eye on the Sun. One orbits ahead of Earth, and one behind. Together, they give us a 3D view of solar storms. It's like having two friends stand on opposite sides of a bonfire to see it from all angles.

5. Hinode, which means "sunrise" in Japanese, studies the Sun's magnetic fields. It has three super-powered telescopes that can see details on the Sun's surface as small as 100 miles across. That's like being able to spot a penny from 100 miles away!

6. The SDO (Solar Dynamics Observatory) takes a picture of the Sun every second! It's like having a non-stop photoshoot with our star. These images help scientists understand how the Sun's activity affects Earth and space weather.

7. IRIS (Interface Region Imaging Spectrograph) looks at a special layer of the Sun's atmosphere. It's trying to solve the mystery of why the Sun's outer atmosphere is much hotter than its surface. Imagine if the air above a campfire was hotter than the fire itself!

8. The PUNCH mission will study how the solar wind leaves the Sun and travels through space. It's like tracking a sneeze from the Sun to see how it spreads through our solar system! PUNCH will help us understand how solar storms form.

9. DKIST (Daniel K. Inouye Solar Telescope) is the world's largest solar telescope. It's not in space, but on a mountain in Hawaii. This telescope can see details on the Sun's surface as small as 18 miles across. It's like having supervision for studying the Sun!

10. The ESA's Proba-2 satellite is small but mighty. It's about the size of a washing machine but packed with instruments to study the Sun. Proba-2 watches for solar flares and helps predict space weather that could affect satellites and power grids on Earth.

11. NASA's TRACERS mission will study the Sun's corona, the mysterious outer layer that's much hotter than the Sun's surface. It's like trying to figure out why the outside of a baked potato is hotter than the inside! TRACERS will help solve this solar mystery.

12. The FIELDS experiment on Parker Solar Probe measures electric and magnetic fields around the Sun. It's like giving the Sun a check-up to understand its "heartbeat" and "pulse." This helps scientists understand how the Sun affects space weather.

13. Solar Orbiter has a special instrument called Metis that creates artificial solar eclipses. It blocks out the bright surface of the Sun so scientists can study the fainter corona. It's like having a mini-eclipse on demand to peek at the Sun's atmosphere!

14. The WISPR instrument on Parker Solar Probe takes pictures of the solar wind. It's like having a super-fast camera that can capture the Sun's "breath" as it blows out into space. These images help us understand how solar wind is born.

15. SOHO has a special instrument called LASCO that watches for coronal mass ejections (CMEs). These are huge eruptions from the Sun that can cause auroras on Earth. LASCO acts like an early warning system for these solar "sneezes."

16. The SWEAP instruments on Parker Solar Probe actually scoop up particles from the Sun's atmosphere to study them. It's like catching snowflakes, but the snowflakes are super-hot and moving incredibly fast! This helps us understand what the Sun is made of.

17. Hinode's X-ray telescope can see hot gases in the Sun's corona. It's like having X-ray vision to look inside the Sun's atmosphere! This helps scientists understand how the Sun creates and releases energy.

18. IRIS can see layers of the Sun's atmosphere that are only about 150 miles thick. That's super thin compared to the whole Sun! It's like being able to see individual layers in a giant cosmic onion.

19. The SPICE instrument on Solar Orbiter measures the temperature and speed of gases flowing in the Sun's atmosphere. It's like taking the Sun's temperature and checking its "wind speed" at the same time!

20. The future EUVST mission will study how energy moves through the Sun's atmosphere. It will use a telescope that can see extreme ultraviolet light. It's like having a special pair of sunglasses that let you see the Sun's hidden energy flows!

Chapter 15: Space Radiation Protection

1. Astronauts wear special space suits with built-in radiation shields. These suits have layers of tough materials that block harmful rays. It's like wearing a suit of armor, but instead of protecting you from swords, it protects you from invisible space rays!

2. The International Space Station has thick walls to shield astronauts from radiation. Some parts of the station have extra shielding, creating "storm shelters" for astronauts during solar flares. It's like having a safe room in a space house!

3. Water is great at blocking radiation, so spacecraft often store their water supplies in the walls. This clever trick provides drinking water and protection at the same time. It's like filling your walls with water balloons to keep you safe!

4. Some spacecraft use aluminum to shield against radiation. Aluminum is light but good at stopping space rays. It's like wearing a hat made of kitchen foil, but much stronger and designed by scientists!

5. Future Mars missions might use plastic containing hydrogen to shield astronauts. Hydrogen is great at stopping radiation. It's like building a space fort out of special plastic blocks to keep the cosmic rays out!

6. Spacecraft heading to the Moon or Mars might have a small room with extra-thick walls. Astronauts could hide here during dangerous solar storms. It's like having a tiny bomb shelter in your spaceship!

7. Scientists are developing special vests for astronauts that can sense radiation and show where it's coming from. It's like having a superhero suit that tells you where danger is so you can avoid it!

8. Some ideas for future spaceships include inflatable radiation shields. These could be blown up like a balloon when needed. Imagine having a bouncy castle in space that protects you from cosmic rays!

9. Earth's magnetic field protects us from a lot of space radiation. Some scientists think we could create a magnetic bubble around a spacecraft for protection. It would be like surrounding your spaceship with an invisible force field!

10. Astronauts on the space station follow a careful schedule to avoid too much radiation exposure. They keep track of how much radiation they've received, like counting how much time you've spent in the sun to avoid sunburn.

11. Some spacecraft use a layer of polyethylene, a type of plastic, to shield against radiation. This material is good at stopping particles from space. It's like wrapping your spaceship in a giant, protective plastic bag!

12. Future space habitats on the Moon or Mars might be built underground. The soil above would act as a natural radiation shield. It's like living in a cool cave house on another world!

13. NASA is researching special materials that can absorb or deflect radiation. Some of these might be used in future spacesuits or ships. Imagine wearing a space jacket that bounces harmful rays away like a mirror!

14. Astronauts take pills containing antioxidants to help their bodies deal with radiation. It's like eating super-powered berries that help your body fight off the effects of space rays!

15. Some scientists suggest using food and poop as radiation shields on long space journeys! The water in food and waste can block radiation. It's a bit yucky, but it's like recycling in space to keep astronauts safe.

16. Spacecraft might one day use superconducting magnets to create a protective bubble against radiation. It would be like having a giant magnet that pushes dangerous particles away from the ship!

17. Thick glass windows on spacecraft help protect astronauts from radiation while still letting them see space. These windows are much thicker than the ones in your house. It's like looking through a shield that's also a window!

18. Some researchers are studying how to use fungi to absorb radiation in space. Certain mushrooms on Earth can eat radiation, so they might help in space too. Imagine having a garden in your spaceship that keeps you safe!

19. Future spacesuits might include a layer that uses electricity to push away charged radiation particles. It would be like having a force field in your clothes that zaps away dangerous space rays!

20. Scientists are looking at how animals like tardigrades survive radiation in space. We might learn how to protect astronauts by studying these tiny, tough creatures. It's like taking lessons from nature's own space explorers!

Chapter 16: Costliest Space Projects

1. The James Webb Space Telescope cost a whopping $10 billion! It's like a time machine that can see the oldest galaxies in the universe. This super-telescope is so powerful, it can spot a bumblebee on the moon from Earth! That's one expensive pair of space binoculars!

2. The International Space Station is the priciest thing humans have ever built in space. It cost over $150 billion! That's like building 150,000 schools. This floating space lab is as big as a football field and has been home to astronauts for over 20 years.

3. NASA's Artemis program, which aims to send humans back to the Moon, might cost $93 billion by 2025. That's as much as buying everyone in New York City a new car! This cosmic project includes a giant rocket called SLS and a spaceship named Orion.

4. The Hubble Space Telescope cost $16 billion to build and maintain. That's like filling a swimming pool with pennies! Hubble has been our eye in the sky for over 30 years, showing us amazing space pictures and helping us understand the universe.

5. The Cassini mission to Saturn cost $3.9 billion. That's like buying 39 million pizzas! Cassini explored Saturn and its moons for 20 years, showing us incredible rings and oceans on distant moons. It was money well spent to explore a giant planet.

6. The Mars Perseverance Rover cost $2.7 billion. That's like buying 270 million ice cream cones! This high-tech robot is exploring Mars, looking for signs of ancient life and collecting samples to be brought back to Earth someday.

7. The Juno spacecraft, which is studying Jupiter, cost $1.1 billion. That's like getting 11 million stuffed animals! Juno is helping us understand the biggest planet in our solar system, diving through Jupiter's stormy clouds and mapping its powerful magnetic field.

8. The Parker Solar Probe, which is studying the Sun up close, cost $1.5 billion. That's like buying 15 million soccer balls! This spacecraft is the fastest human-made object ever, zooming through the Sun's atmosphere to help us understand our star.

9. The Curiosity Rover on Mars cost $2.5 billion. That's like getting 25 million books for your library! Curiosity has been exploring Mars since 2012, climbing mountains and studying rocks to learn about the Red Planet's history.

10. The New Horizons spacecraft, which visited Pluto, cost $720 million. That's like buying 7 million bicycles! This plucky probe traveled for 9 years to give us our first close-up look at Pluto and is now exploring even more distant objects.

11. The Lunar Reconnaissance Orbiter, which maps the Moon, cost $504 million. That's like getting 5 million toy robots! This orbiter has been circling the Moon since 2009, taking super detailed pictures to help plan future lunar missions.

12. The OSIRIS-REx mission to asteroid Bennu cost $800 million. That's like buying 8 million kites! This spacecraft traveled to an asteroid, grabbed some samples, and is bringing them back to Earth for scientists to study.

13. The Mars Reconnaissance Orbiter cost $720 million. That's like getting 7 million board games! This orbiter has been taking amazing high-resolution pictures of Mars since 2006, helping us choose landing sites for rovers and understand Martian weather.

14. The Chandra X-ray Observatory cost $2.5 billion. That's like buying 25 million pairs of sneakers! This space telescope looks at X-rays from space, showing us exploding stars, black holes, and other cosmic wonders invisible to our eyes.

15. The Europa Clipper mission, set to launch in 2024, might cost $4.25 billion. That's like buying 42 million skateboards! This spacecraft will study Jupiter's moon Europa, which might have an ocean under its icy surface where alien life could exist.

16. The GOES-R weather satellite series cost $10.8 billion. That's like getting 108 million umbrellas! These satellites help predict weather on Earth, tracking storms and giving us those cool satellite images we see on weather forecasts.

17. The GPS satellite constellation cost about $12 billion. That's like buying 120 million compasses! These satellites help us navigate on Earth, whether we're using our phones for directions or pilots are flying planes.

18. The Psyche mission to a metal asteroid will cost about $967 million. That's like buying 9 million telescopes! This spacecraft will visit an asteroid that might be the exposed core of an early planet, teaching us about how planets form.

19. The JUICE mission to Jupiter's moons will cost about $1.5 billion. That's like getting 15 million globes! This European spacecraft will study three of Jupiter's largest moons, looking for potential homes for alien life.

20. The WFIRST space telescope might cost $3.2 billion. That's like buying 32 million cameras! This future telescope will study dark energy, exoplanets, and take wide-field pictures of the universe, helping us understand cosmic mysteries.

Chapter 17: Beyond Solar System Explorers

1. Voyager 1 became the first spacecraft to leave our solar system in 2012. It's now in interstellar space, over 14 billion miles from Earth! That's so far, it takes light 21 hours to reach it. Voyager 1 is like an explorer who's stepped off the edge of our cosmic map.

2. Voyager 2 followed its twin into interstellar space in 2018. It's the only spacecraft to visit all four giant planets: Jupiter, Saturn, Uranus, and Neptune. Imagine taking a road trip to visit all the big kids in the neighborhood before leaving town forever!

3. Both Voyager spacecraft carry golden records with sounds and images from Earth. These are like time capsules of our planet. If aliens ever find them, they'll learn about Earth's life and cultures. It's our cosmic message in a bottle!

4. Pioneer 10 was the first spacecraft to travel through the asteroid belt and visit Jupiter. It's now heading out of our solar system. Pioneer 10 carries a plaque with a map showing aliens how to find Earth. It's like leaving our cosmic address for space visitors!

5. Pioneer 11 visited Jupiter and Saturn before starting its journey out of the solar system. It was the first spacecraft to see Saturn's rings up close. Now it's racing its twin, Pioneer 10, into interstellar space. It's like a slow-motion space race that's been going for decades!

6. New Horizons, famous for visiting Pluto, is on its way out of the solar system. It's exploring the Kuiper Belt, a region of icy objects beyond Neptune. New Horizons is like a tourist taking pictures of the solar system's backyard before leaving town.

7. The Voyager spacecraft are so far away, they see stars in slightly different positions than we do on Earth. This change in perspective is called parallax. It's like how things seem to move when you look out a car window, but on a much bigger scale!

8. Voyager 1's cameras were turned off after it took the famous "Pale Blue Dot" picture of Earth in 1990. Now it listens to space plasma and magnetic fields. It's like closing your eyes and using your other senses to explore a new place.

9. Both Voyagers use plutonium power sources that will run out around 2025. After that, they'll keep flying silently through space forever. They're like bottles tossed into a cosmic ocean, carrying messages from Earth for countless years.

10. The edge of our solar system is called the heliopause. It's where the Sun's influence ends and interstellar space begins. The Voyagers crossed this boundary, like explorers stepping from familiar waters into a vast, unknown sea.

11. Pioneer 10 and 11 have both fallen silent, but they continue their journey into interstellar space. We can no longer hear them, but they carry humanity's first messages to the stars. They're like silent ambassadors from Earth, eternally traveling outward.

12. The Voyager spacecraft are traveling in different directions out of the solar system. Voyager 1 is heading towards the constellation Ophiuchus, while Voyager 2 is moving towards Telescopium. It's like two friends leaving home and going on different adventures.

13. In about 40,000 years, Voyager 1 will pass within 1.6 light-years of the star Gliese 445. That's the closest it will get to another star. It's like planning a meeting with a neighbor that won't happen for thousands of generations!

14. The Voyagers' golden records contain 115 images, natural sounds, music from different cultures, and greetings in 55 languages. If aliens find them, they'll get a snapshot of life on Earth. It's like making the ultimate mix tape for the universe!

15. New Horizons might be the last spacecraft to leave our solar system for a long time. Future missions will likely focus on exploring our own cosmic backyard more thoroughly. New Horizons is like the last runner in a long relay race into interstellar space.

16. The Voyagers discovered many new moons around the giant planets before leaving the solar system. They were like celestial explorers, mapping out our cosmic neighborhood before venturing into the unknown.

17. As the Voyagers left the solar system, they noticed the solar wind (particles from the Sun) get weaker and cosmic rays from deep space get stronger. It was like feeling a cool breeze as they left the warmth of our solar "home."

18. The Voyagers' journey out of the solar system taught us that the edge of our cosmic neighborhood isn't a clear line, but a bubbly, frothy boundary. It's like discovering that the fence around your yard is actually a giant, wobbly bubble!

19. Even though they've left the solar system, the Voyagers won't reach another star system for about 40,000 years. Space is really, really big! It's like leaving your house and taking 40,000 years to reach your neighbor's front door.

20. Scientists think there might be a giant bubble around our entire solar system called the Oort Cloud. The Voyagers won't reach its inner edge for about 300 years. It's like discovering your backyard is actually thousands of times bigger than you thought!

Chapter 18: Spacecraft Power Generation

1. Many spacecraft use solar panels to make electricity. These panels are like big, flat sunflowers that drink in sunlight and turn it into power. The International Space Station has solar panels as long as a football field! They provide enough electricity to power 40 houses on Earth.

2. Some deep space probes use RTGs (Radioisotope Thermoelectric Generators). These are like special batteries that use heat from radioactive material to make electricity. The Voyager spacecraft have been powered by RTGs for over 40 years as they explore beyond our solar system!

3. The Juno spacecraft orbiting Jupiter uses giant solar panels to make power. But Jupiter is really far from the Sun, so Juno's panels had to be super big - about the size of a basketball court! It's like having a huge solar-powered calculator studying the biggest planet.

4. The Parker Solar Probe, which studies the Sun up close, has a clever cooling system for its solar panels. They hide behind a special shield when it gets too hot, then pop out to catch some rays when it's safe. It's like playing peek-a-boo with the Sun!

5. The Mars rovers use solar panels to power their adventures on the Red Planet. But Martian dust can cover the panels, so the rovers do a little dance to shake it off. Imagine doing a shimmy to clean your shirt - that's how Mars rovers keep their solar panels clean!

6. Some satellites use fuel cells to make electricity. These combine hydrogen and oxygen to produce power and water. It's like having a mini power plant that makes its own water! Astronauts on the Space Shuttle used to drink the water made by their fuel cells.

7. The Cassini spacecraft, which explored Saturn, used RTGs because solar panels wouldn't work so far from the Sun. Its power source was like a cosmic campfire, providing warmth and electricity for Cassini's 20-year journey around the ringed planet.

8. The Hubble Space Telescope gets its power from the Sun, but in a special way. It has solar panels that charge batteries while it's in sunlight. Then, when it's in Earth's shadow, it uses the stored battery power. It's like filling up a cosmic piggy bank with sunlight!

9. Some spacecraft use a trick called "gravity assist" to save power. They swing by planets to get a speed boost, like a cosmic slingshot. This means they need less fuel and can use smaller power sources. It's like getting a push on a swing to go higher and faster!

10. The New Horizons spacecraft, which visited Pluto, uses an RTG for power. Even billions of miles from the Sun, it has enough electricity to run its instruments and send messages home. It's like having a tiny nuclear battery that lasts for decades!

11. Future spacecraft might use small nuclear reactors for power. These could provide lots of electricity for long missions to Mars or the outer planets. Imagine having a power plant the size of a trash can that could run a whole spaceship!

12. The BepiColombo mission to Mercury uses both solar power and ion engines. The ion engines use electricity to push out charged particles, moving the spacecraft. It's like having a super-efficient electric car engine that works in space!

13. Some CubeSats, which are tiny satellites, use small solar panels and batteries. They're so efficient that they can run on about as much power as a bright light bulb! It's like powering a tiny space explorer with the same energy you use to read a book at night.

14. The International Space Station's solar panels move to follow the Sun as it orbits Earth. They're always trying to catch the most sunlight, like sunflowers turning to face the Sun. This helps the station generate enough power for all its experiments and life support systems.

15. The Rosetta spacecraft, which visited a comet, had to hibernate for part of its journey to save power. It's solar panels weren't getting enough light, so it took a long nap. Imagine going to sleep for two years to save energy - that's what Rosetta did!

16. Some spacecraft use thermoelectric generators, which turn heat directly into electricity. They work great in space where it's very cold on one side of the spacecraft and warm on the other. It's like making power from the difference between a hot cup of cocoa and an ice cube!

17. The Mars Helicopter, Ingenuity, uses a small solar panel to charge its batteries. It needs to save up enough power during the day for a short flight. It's like a toy drone that charges up in the sun before taking a quick spin on another planet!

18. Future spacecraft might use advanced solar cells that work better in low light. This could help power missions to the outer planets where sunlight is weak. Imagine having super eyes that can see in the dark - these solar cells would be like super power collectors!

19. Some proposed spacecraft designs use large, thin sails pushed by sunlight or laser beams. These light sails wouldn't need fuel, just the pressure of light to move. It's like having a giant kite in space, blown by a breeze of light!

20. The JUICE mission to Jupiter's moons will use huge solar panels to work in the dim sunlight near Jupiter. These panels could cover a large classroom! It's like needing a really big net to catch enough sunlight to power your space adventure when you're far from the Sun.

Chapter 19: First Planetary Orbiters

1. Mariner 9 became the first spacecraft to orbit another planet when it reached Mars in 1971. It arrived during a huge dust storm that covered the whole planet! Mariner 9 patiently waited for the storm to clear, then took amazing pictures of Mars' surface. It was like unveiling a cosmic mystery!

2. The Soviet spacecraft Mars 2 also reached Mars orbit in 1971, just days after Mariner 9. But its lander crashed on the surface. Mars 2 showed us how tricky it is to explore other planets. It's like trying to land a paper airplane on a moving target millions of miles away!

3. Pioneer Venus 1 became the first spacecraft to orbit Venus in 1978. It discovered that Venus has weird double hurricanes at its poles! Pioneer Venus 1 taught us that our nearest neighbor planet is very different from Earth. It's like finding out your next-door neighbor is an alien!

4. Messenger became the first spacecraft to orbit Mercury in 2011. It took over six years to get there! Messenger had to do a cosmic dance, flying past Earth, Venus, and Mercury multiple times to slow down enough to enter orbit. It's like playing interplanetary hopscotch!

5. Galileo was the first spacecraft to orbit Jupiter, arriving in 1995. It discovered that Jupiter's moon Europa might have an ocean under its icy surface! Galileo showed us that the giant planets have fascinating moons. It's like finding a whole family of new worlds to explore!

6. Cassini became the first spacecraft to orbit Saturn in 2004. It saw amazing things like ice geysers on the moon Enceladus and lakes on Titan! Cassini spent 13 years exploring Saturn and its moons. It's like taking a really long field trip to the most spectacular science museum ever!

7. NEAR Shoemaker was the first spacecraft to orbit an asteroid, reaching Eros in 2000. It even landed on Eros at the end of its mission! NEAR showed us that even small space rocks can be fascinating worlds. It's like studying a pebble and finding out it's full of secrets!

8. Mars Global Surveyor orbited Mars for nine years, longer than any other spacecraft at the time. It took so many pictures, we could make a super detailed map of Mars. It's like drawing the best treasure map ever, but for a whole planet!

9. Magellan was the first spacecraft to map almost all of Venus using radar. It could see through Venus' thick clouds to map mountains and valleys. Magellan was like a cosmic x-ray machine, showing us the hidden face of our sister planet!

10. Lunar Orbiter 1 became the first spacecraft to orbit the Moon in 1966. It took detailed pictures to help choose landing spots for Apollo astronauts. It was like a space scout, finding the best camping spots on the Moon for humans to visit!

11. Dawn was the first spacecraft to orbit two different bodies beyond Earth. It visited the asteroid Vesta, then went on to orbit the dwarf planet Ceres. Dawn was like a cosmic tourist, visiting different stops on a grand tour of the asteroid belt!

12. Mars Odyssey has been orbiting Mars longer than any other spacecraft - since 2001! It's like a tireless Martian weatherman, reporting on Mars' climate and helping other Mars missions communicate with Earth.

13. Juno is the first spacecraft to orbit Jupiter's poles. It flies over Jupiter's cloud tops, closer than any spacecraft before. Juno is like a cosmic acrobat, doing daring dives to study the giant planet's powerful storms and magnetic fields.

14. MAVEN is studying how Mars lost its atmosphere by orbiting the planet and sometimes dipping into its upper air. It's like a detective trying to solve the mystery of Mars' missing air by flying through the crime scene!

15. BepiColombo will be the first European mission to orbit Mercury when it arrives in 2025. It had to take the scenic route, flying past Earth, Venus, and Mercury multiple times to slow down. It's like playing cosmic pinball to reach the innermost planet!

16. Akatsuki is Japan's first spacecraft to orbit another planet. After missing Venus on its first try, it orbited the Sun for five years before successfully entering Venus orbit in 2015. It's like getting a second chance at a really hard video game level!

17. New Horizons flew past Pluto in 2015, giving us our first close-up look at this distant world. While it didn't orbit Pluto, it showed us that even the farthest planets can be amazing. It's like finally getting to meet a pen pal you've been writing to for years!

18. The Mars Reconnaissance Orbiter has the most powerful camera ever sent to another planet. It can see objects on Mars as small as a kitchen table! It's like having superhero vision to spot tiny details on the Red Planet.

19. India's Mars Orbiter Mission, also called Mangalyaan, reached Mars orbit on its first try in 2014. India became the first country to do this on its first attempt! It's like scoring a hole-in-one on your very first game of golf - in space!

20. The European Space Agency's Mars Express has been orbiting Mars since 2003. It discovered underground water ice on Mars! Mars Express is like a cosmic water diviner, finding hidden resources that future Mars explorers might use.

Chapter 20: Comet and Asteroid Chasers

1. The Stardust spacecraft was like a cosmic catcher's mitt! It flew through the tail of comet Wild 2, collecting tiny dust particles in a special gel. When it returned to Earth, scientists found bits of stardust older than our solar system. It's like catching pieces of the universe's history!

2. Japan's Hayabusa spacecraft was the first to bring back samples from an asteroid. It landed on asteroid Itokawa, fired a bullet into the surface, and caught the dust that flew up. Imagine using a BB gun to collect space rocks!

3. NASA's OSIRIS-REx played tag with asteroid Bennu. It briefly touched the asteroid's surface with a robotic arm, blasting it with air to stir up rocks and dust. Then it quickly scooped up the samples and flew away. It's like a high-speed game of "grab and go" in space!

4. The Deep Impact mission was like a cosmic collision experiment. It sent a copper "impactor" crashing into comet Tempel 1 at high speed. The main spacecraft watched the explosion, learning about the comet's insides. It's like cracking open a space egg to see what's inside!

5. Rosetta was the first spacecraft to orbit a comet. It followed comet 67P for two years, watching it change as it got closer to the Sun. Rosetta even dropped a little lander called Philae onto the comet's surface. It's like becoming best friends with a dirty snowball in space!

6. The Lucy mission is on a journey to visit seven different Trojan asteroids. These asteroids share Jupiter's orbit around the Sun. Lucy will be like a cosmic tourist, taking a grand tour of these ancient space rocks over 12 years.

7. NASA's DART mission was like a game of interplanetary billiards. It deliberately crashed into the asteroid Dimorphos to see if it could change its orbit. This test could help protect Earth from dangerous asteroids in the future. It's like practicing how to nudge space rocks away from Earth!

8. Hayabusa2, another Japanese mission, visited asteroid Ryugu. It shot a copper bullet into the asteroid and collected the debris. It even created an artificial crater with an explosive device! Hayabusa2 was like a cosmic archaeologist, digging for space treasures.

9. The Comet Interceptor mission will wait in space for a new comet to appear, then zoom off to study it. It's like a patient hunter, always ready to chase after a new, exciting cosmic prey. This spacecraft could give us our first look at a pristine comet from the outer solar system!

10. The Near Earth Asteroid Rendezvous (NEAR) Shoemaker spacecraft orbited asteroid Eros for a year before landing on it. It was the first spacecraft to land on an asteroid. Imagine parallel parking on a giant, lumpy space potato!

11. The Dawn mission visited both asteroid Vesta and dwarf planet Ceres. It was the first spacecraft to orbit two different bodies beyond Earth. Dawn was like a space explorer on a road trip, visiting the biggest "rest stops" in the asteroid belt.

12. Hera, a European mission, will visit asteroid Dimorphos after DART's impact. It will be like a detective, studying the crime scene after DART's cosmic collision to see how well we can deflect asteroids. Hera is helping us learn how to protect Earth from space rocks!

13. The Destiny+ mission will visit asteroid Phaethon, which creates the Geminid meteor shower on Earth. It's like chasing the source of nature's most spectacular fireworks show! Destiny+ will help us understand where shooting stars come from.

14. NASA's Psyche mission will visit an asteroid made mostly of metal. Scientists think it might be the exposed core of an early planet. It's like finding a giant ball of iron floating in space! Psyche could teach us about how planets form.

15. The CAESAR mission (if selected) would bring back a piece of comet 67P/Churyumov-Gerasimenko to Earth. It's like going on a long journey to collect a souvenir from a cosmic snowball! This could help us understand how comets and our solar system formed.

16. China's Tianwen-2 mission plans to visit asteroid Kamo'oalewa, collect samples, and then fly to a comet. It's like a space explorer with a very busy travel itinerary, hopping between different kinds of space objects!

17. The NEO Surveyor mission will search for asteroids that might be dangerous to Earth. It's like a space safety inspector, keeping an eye out for cosmic rocks that could cause trouble. NEO Surveyor will help us find asteroids before they find us!

18. The Comet Nucleus Tour (CONTOUR) was designed to visit three different comets. Sadly, it was lost after launch. But its ambitious plan was like a cosmic road trip, trying to visit multiple comets on one tank of gas!

19. The REXIS instrument on OSIRIS-REx used X-rays to study what asteroid Bennu is made of. It's like having X-ray vision to see inside a space rock without touching it! REXIS helped scientists choose where to collect samples on Bennu.

20. The MMX mission will visit Mars' moons Phobos and Deimos, and return samples from Phobos. Some scientists think these moons might be captured asteroids. It's like solving a cosmic mystery: are Mars' moons really asteroids in disguise?

Chapter 21: Extreme Temperature Survival

1. The Parker Solar Probe gets closer to the Sun than any spacecraft before! It uses a special heat shield made of carbon to protect itself. This shield is so good at its job, it keeps the spacecraft cool even when the front is hot enough to melt steel. It's like having the world's best umbrella on a really, really hot day!

2. Spacecraft visiting icy moons like Europa need to stay warm in the freezing cold of outer space. They use special heaters and wrap themselves in blankets made of gold foil. It's like wearing a super-powered winter coat that keeps you toasty even on the coldest day ever!

3. The Venus Express spacecraft had to deal with temperatures hot enough to melt lead! It used special mirrors to reflect away the heat and kept its instruments in a box cooled by space itself. Imagine having a lunchbox that stays cool by opening it towards the coldness of space!

4. Mars rovers like Perseverance use a trick called a "heat switch" to stay warm at night. It's like a thermos that can turn on and off. During the day, it collects heat, and at night, it releases that heat to keep the rover's parts warm in the freezing Martian night.

5. The James Webb Space Telescope needs to stay super cold to see faint heat from distant stars. It uses a giant sunshield the size of a tennis court to block heat from the Sun, Earth, and Moon. It's like sitting in the shade of the biggest beach umbrella ever!

6. Spacecraft orbiting Earth, like weather satellites, deal with extreme temperature changes as they move from sunlight to Earth's shadow. They use special paint that changes color with temperature to help control heat. It's like wearing a mood ring that keeps you comfortable!

7. The Messenger spacecraft that studied Mercury had to withstand temperatures up to 427°C (800°F)! It used special ceramic fabric sunshades to protect itself. Imagine wearing oven mitts that could protect you from the hottest oven in the world!

8. Voyager 1 and 2, exploring the outer solar system, use radioactive decay to generate heat and power. As they get farther from the Sun, they shut down unnecessary systems to conserve energy. It's like putting on extra layers and taking a nap to stay warm on a long, cold journey.

9. The Curiosity rover on Mars uses a nuclear power source that gives off heat as a byproduct. This helps keep the rover warm in the cold Martian nights. It's like having a tiny, safe nuclear campfire that never goes out!

10. Spacecraft visiting comets, like Rosetta, need to protect themselves from tiny, high-speed dust particles. They use special shielding and can turn to present their toughest side towards the dust. It's like hiding behind a shield in a cosmic snowball fight!

11. The International Space Station uses ammonia-filled pipes to move heat from inside to outside. The pipes lead to giant radiators that release the heat into space. It's like having a giant air conditioner that dumps the heat into the biggest freezer ever - space itself!

12. The Lunar Reconnaissance Orbiter uses louvers, which are like adjustable blinds, to control its temperature. When it's hot, the louvers open to let heat out. When it's cold, they close to keep heat in. It's like having magic windows that know when you need to cool down or warm up!

13. Some Mars landers use a phase change material, similar to wax, that melts during the hot day and freezes at night. This helps keep the spacecraft's temperature steady. It's like having a ice pack that melts to cool you down, then freezes again to warm you up!

14. The New Horizons spacecraft, which visited Pluto, uses layers of insulation and small heaters to stay warm in the outer solar system. It's like wearing many layers of clothes and having tiny hand warmers all over your body to stay cozy in the coldest place you can imagine!

15. The Juno spacecraft orbiting Jupiter is protected from intense radiation by a titanium vault. This vault also helps protect sensitive electronics from extreme temperature changes. It's like having a superhero suit that protects you from both heat and cold!

16. Solar panels on spacecraft can get very hot in direct sunlight. Some spacecraft use them as shields, positioning them to protect other parts of the spacecraft from the Sun's heat. It's like using a big sun hat to shade your whole body!

17. The BepiColombo mission to Mercury uses a combination of ceramic and titanium to withstand extreme heat. Its solar panels can tilt to avoid overheating. Imagine having an indestructible umbrella that you can adjust to always keep you in the shade!

18. Spacecraft that land on asteroids, like OSIRIS-REx, need to handle rapid temperature changes as the asteroid rotates. They use materials that can expand and contract without breaking. It's like wearing clothes that can quickly change from a winter coat to a t-shirt!

19. The Mars 2020 Perseverance rover uses a system called MOXIE to make oxygen from Mars' atmosphere. This system gets very hot, so it's insulated like a tiny oven inside the rover. It's like having a small bread oven inside your car that doesn't make the rest of the car hot!

20. Future spacecraft might use "sunglasses" made of electrochromic materials. These can darken when it's too bright and hot, and lighten when more heat is needed. It's like having windows that automatically tint to keep you comfortable, no matter how bright it is outside!

Chapter 22: Heaviest Space Cargo

1. The Saturn V rocket, used in the Apollo missions, could lift 310,000 pounds to orbit! That's as heavy as 31 school buses. This mighty rocket carried everything needed to send astronauts to the Moon, including the lunar lander and command module. It was like a cosmic moving truck for Moon explorers!

2. The Space Shuttle could carry 65,000 pounds to orbit. That's the weight of about 8 elephants! It had a huge cargo bay that could fit a school bus. The Shuttle delivered satellites, space station parts, and even the Hubble Space Telescope. It was like a space delivery truck!

3. The Falcon Heavy rocket can lift 141,000 pounds to orbit. That's as heavy as a whole blue whale! On its first test flight, it carried a red Tesla car into space. Imagine sending your toy car on a cosmic road trip!

4. Russia's Proton rocket can lift 51,000 pounds to orbit. That's like carrying 25 grand pianos into space! It has launched heavy satellites and even parts of the International Space Station. The Proton is like a cosmic weightlifter, flexing its muscles to lift huge space gadgets.

5. The Delta IV Heavy rocket can carry 63,000 pounds to orbit. That's the weight of about 9 pickup trucks! This powerful rocket has launched spy satellites and a test version of NASA's Orion spacecraft. It's like a secret agent of rockets, carrying mysterious payloads to space.

6. China's Long March 5 rocket can lift 55,000 pounds to orbit. That's as heavy as 5 adult hippos! It has launched space station modules and a mission to Mars. The Long March 5 is like a cosmic crane, hoisting huge pieces of China's space dreams into the sky.

7. The Ariane 5 rocket, used by Europe, can carry 44,000 pounds to orbit. That's about the weight of 4 tyrannosaurus rex dinosaurs! It often launches two big satellites at once. Imagine giving two space robots a piggyback ride to orbit!

8. NASA's new SLS (Space Launch System) rocket is designed to carry 209,000 pounds to orbit. That's like lifting 20 fully grown elephants! This massive rocket will send astronauts and cargo to the Moon and maybe even Mars. It's the ultimate cosmic moving van!

9. The Soviet Energia rocket could lift 220,000 pounds to orbit. That's as heavy as a whole blue whale and its baby! It only flew twice before being retired. The Energia was like a super-strong but short-lived cosmic athlete, setting records before hanging up its space boots.

10. SpaceX's Starship, still being developed, aims to carry 330,000 pounds to orbit. That's like launching 16 school buses at once! If successful, it could be the most powerful rocket ever. Starship is like a cosmic sumo wrestler, planning to out-lift all other rockets.

11. The Titan IV rocket could lift 47,800 pounds to orbit. That's about the weight of 4 African elephants! It was used to launch heavy spy satellites and space probes. The Titan IV was like a secret space delivery service, carrying mystery packages to orbit.

12. Japan's H-IIA rocket can carry 22,000 pounds to orbit. That's like lifting 11 small cars! It has launched satellites and space probes, including a mission to Venus. The H-IIA is like a cosmic sushi chef, carefully placing Japan's space dreams into perfect orbits.

13. The Atlas V rocket can lift up to 41,500 pounds to orbit. That's about as heavy as 4 big trucks! It has launched Mars rovers and many important satellites. Atlas V is like a reliable space taxi, always ready to give your satellite a lift to orbit.

14. India's GSLV Mk III rocket can carry 17,600 pounds to orbit. That's like lifting an entire school bus! It has launched communication satellites and could send Indian astronauts to space. The GSLV Mk III is India's cosmic rickshaw, carrying big dreams to the stars.

15. The Pegasus rocket is launched from an airplane and can carry 1,000 pounds to orbit. That's like lifting a grand piano! It's perfect for small satellites. Imagine giving your toy airplane super powers to launch real satellites into space!

16. The Electron rocket can lift 660 pounds to orbit. That's about the weight of a big horse! It's designed for small satellites and launches often. The Electron is like a cosmic courier service, making quick, regular deliveries to space.

17. The Vega rocket from Europe can carry 3,300 pounds to orbit. That's as heavy as a big SUV! It's great for launching Earth observation satellites. Vega is like a space mountain climber, specialized in reaching certain orbits other rockets find tricky.

18. The Soyuz rocket, a space veteran, can lift about 16,500 pounds to orbit. That's like carrying 8 cows to space! It has launched thousands of missions, including many trips to the space station. Soyuz is the reliable old horse of the space race, always ready for another ride.

19. The Antares rocket can carry 17,600 pounds to orbit. That's about the weight of 4 hippos! It's used to send cargo to the International Space Station. Antares is like a space grocery delivery truck, bringing fresh supplies to astronauts.

20. The New Glenn rocket, still being developed, aims to lift 99,000 pounds to orbit. That's as heavy as 9 school buses! It's named after John Glenn, the first American to orbit Earth. New Glenn wants to be like its namesake - a pioneer in space exploration!

Chapter 23: Spacecraft Formations

1. The Magnetospheric Multiscale Mission uses four identical spacecraft flying in a pyramid shape. They dance around Earth, changing their formation to study our planet's magnetic field. It's like a cosmic ballet, with four space dancers moving in perfect sync!

2. The GRACE satellites worked as a pair to measure Earth's gravity. They flew 220 kilometers apart, constantly measuring the distance between them. When they flew over areas with more mass, gravity pulled them closer together. It's like playing a game of cosmic tug-of-war!

3. The Swarm mission uses three satellites to study Earth's magnetic field. Two fly side by side, while the third orbits higher up. Together, they create a 3D map of our planet's magnetism. Imagine three space artists working together to paint a picture of Earth's invisible shield!

4. NASA's CYGNSS constellation has eight small satellites that work together to peek inside hurricanes. They spread out around Earth, always ready to watch storms form. It's like having a team of tiny storm chasers in space, keeping an eye on the weather for us!

5. The COSMIC-2 mission uses six satellites to study Earth's atmosphere. They receive signals from GPS satellites that have traveled through the atmosphere, revealing its properties. It's like having a team of space weather reporters, telling us what's happening high above our heads!

6. The Iridium satellite constellation has 66 satellites working together to provide phone service anywhere on Earth. They form a web around our planet, passing calls from one satellite to another. Imagine a game of cosmic telephone, with satellites passing messages around the world!

7. The Planet Labs' Dove satellites work in a huge team of over 100 small spacecraft. They photograph Earth every day, showing us how our planet changes. It's like having a flock of space pigeons, each taking pictures and sending them back to us!

8. The Starlink satellites fly in large groups to provide internet access around the world. They look like a string of pearls moving across the night sky. Imagine a cosmic game of connect-the-dots, with each satellite being a dot that brings internet to people below!

9. The STEREO mission used two spacecraft to get a 3D view of the Sun. One flew ahead of Earth in its orbit, while the other lagged behind. Together, they gave us our first complete view of our star. It's like having two cosmic photographers taking pictures of the Sun from different angles!

10. The Cluster mission uses four spacecraft flying in a tetrahedral formation to study Earth's magnetosphere. They can change their spacing from 100 to 10,000 kilometers apart. Imagine four space explorers holding corners of a giant, invisible pyramid around Earth!

11. The TanDEM-X and TerraSAR-X satellites fly in close formation to create 3D maps of Earth. They orbit just a few hundred meters apart, working together like cosmic cartographers. It's like having two space artists drawing the most detailed picture of Earth ever made!

12. The PROBA-3 mission will use two spacecraft to create an artificial solar eclipse in space. One will act as the Moon, blocking the Sun's bright surface so the other can study its corona. Imagine playing a cosmic game of hide-and-seek to uncover the Sun's secrets!

13. The QB50 project launched 50 tiny CubeSats to study Earth's lower thermosphere. These little spacecraft work as a team, spread out to take measurements all around our planet. It's like having a swarm of space bees, buzzing around Earth to learn about its upper atmosphere!

14. The Orbiting Carbon Observatory-3 works with other satellites to study Earth's carbon cycle. It measures carbon dioxide from the International Space Station while others watch from different orbits. Imagine a team of space detectives, each looking for clues about Earth's changing climate!

15. The A-Train is a group of satellites that fly one after another, like a train in space. They all cross the equator within minutes of each other, each studying different parts of Earth's climate. It's like a cosmic conga line, with each satellite dancing to the rhythm of Earth's weather!

16. The Landsat satellites work in pairs to continuously monitor Earth's surface. As one gets old, a new one is launched to take over, ensuring we always have eyes on our changing planet. It's like a team of space guards, always keeping watch over Earth's landscapes!

17. The Global Precipitation Measurement mission uses a network of satellites to track rain and snow worldwide. They work together to give us a complete picture of Earth's water cycle every three hours. Imagine a team of space weather reporters, always ready with the latest forecast!

18. The THEMIS mission used five satellites to study Earth's auroras. They lined up in space to watch how particles from the Sun create these beautiful light shows. It's like having five celestial photographers capturing the most spectacular light show in the solar system!

19. The LISA Pathfinder mission tested technology for future gravitational wave detectors in space. It used two cubes floating inside the spacecraft, watching how they moved. In the future, three spacecraft will do this over millions of kilometers! It's like playing the world's biggest game of cosmic Ping-Pong!

20. The Artemis program will use multiple spacecraft working together to return humans to the Moon. This includes the Orion capsule, a lunar lander, and the Gateway space station orbiting the Moon. Imagine a cosmic relay race, with different spacecraft passing astronauts from Earth to the Moon's surface!

Chapter 24: Planetary Landing Techniques

1. When the Mars rovers land, they use a "sky crane" technique. The spacecraft lowers the rover on cables while hovering above the surface. It's like a cosmic game of crane claw, gently placing the rover on Mars before flying away!

2. The Apollo lunar landers used rocket engines to slow down. As they approached the Moon, they fired engines to gently lower themselves to the surface. Imagine riding a rocket-powered elevator down to the Moon!

3. Some spacecraft use airbags to land safely. They inflate big balloon-like bags around the spacecraft just before landing. It's like wrapping yourself in giant bubble wrap before jumping off a high dive!

4. The Huygens probe used parachutes to land on Saturn's moon Titan. It floated down through Titan's thick atmosphere like a cosmic dandelion seed. Imagine parachuting onto an alien world with lakes of liquid methane!

5. The Perseverance rover used a combination of parachutes, rockets, and a sky crane to land on Mars. It's like a three-act play of landing techniques, each part working together to set the rover down gently.

6. When landing on a comet, the Philae lander used harpoons to anchor itself. The comet's gravity is so weak, without the harpoons, Philae might have bounced off! It's like playing darts with a tiny space world.

7. The Soviet Venera landers used special materials to withstand Venus' intense heat and pressure. They slowed down with parachutes but had to survive a hard landing. Imagine building a spacecraft tough enough to land in an oven!

8. SpaceX's Starship is designed to land using its engines, flipping itself vertical just before touchdown. It's like a rocket doing a last-minute somersault before gently setting down on its tail.

9. The Chinese Chang'e-5 mission used a two-part lander to visit the Moon. One part stayed in orbit while the other landed. It's like having a cosmic buddy system - one friend stays in the car while the other runs into the store!

10. NASA's OSIRIS-REx spacecraft didn't fully land on asteroid Bennu. Instead, it did a "touch-and-go" maneuver, briefly touching down to collect samples. It's like playing the fastest game of tag ever with a space rock!

11. The Mars Phoenix lander used rocket engines to slow down, then legs to absorb the impact of landing. It's like jumping off a high dive and landing on a giant spring-loaded stool!

12. Future missions to Jupiter's moon Europa might use a "tuneable landing system" with legs that can adjust to unknown terrain. It's like having a spacecraft with legs that can tiptoe or stomp, depending on what it finds!

13. The Soviet Mars 3 lander used a combination of parachutes and rocket engines to land on Mars. Although it only worked for a few seconds, it was the first successful soft landing on Mars. Imagine being the first to gently step onto a new world!

14. The Hayabusa2 spacecraft used tiny explosive charges to create a crater on asteroid Ryugu before landing. It's like setting off the world's smallest firework to make a landing spot on a space rock!

15. NASA's InSight lander used parachutes and rockets to land on Mars, then deployed solar panels shaped like fans. It's like a cosmic flower blooming on the red Martian soil!

16. The Rosetta mission's Philae lander bounced when it first touched down on comet 67P. Its harpoons didn't fire, so it took three bounces before settling. Imagine playing basketball on a comet - every bounce takes you higher!

17. Future missions to Saturn's moon Enceladus might use a "crawling" lander to navigate the icy, cracked surface. It would be like sending a cosmic crab to explore an alien ice world!

18. The Soviet Venera 7 was the first spacecraft to land on Venus and transmit data. It used parachutes but still hit the surface hard. Imagine dropping your toy spaceship into a pressure cooker - that's how tough Venera 7 had to be!

19. NASA's proposed Dragonfly mission to Saturn's moon Titan would use rotors, like a helicopter, to fly from place to place after landing. It's like having a cosmic drone explore an alien world!

20. The NEAR Shoemaker spacecraft wasn't designed to land, but engineers decided to try anyway at the end of its mission to asteroid Eros. Surprisingly, it survived! It's like accidentally sticking a perfect landing in gymnastics.

Conclusion

Wow, space cadets! What an incredible journey we've had through the universe of spacecraft! From the tiniest space explorers to the mightiest rockets, we've zoomed across our solar system and beyond. We've discovered how spacecraft battle extreme temperatures, snatch samples from asteroids, and even use the power of the Sun to sail through space!

Remember, every spacecraft, big or small, is a triumph of human imagination and ingenuity. They're our eyes, ears, and hands in the vast cosmic ocean, helping us unravel the mysteries of planets, moons, and distant stars. Who knows? Maybe one day, you'll be the brilliant mind behind a new spacecraft design, or the brave astronaut piloting a mission to Mars!

As we've learned, the future of space exploration is super exciting. With shape-shifting ships, cosmic elevators, and robots that can think for themselves, the possibilities are as endless as the universe itself. So keep looking up at the night sky, and dream big!

Whether you're fascinated by space toilets or thrilled by the idea of growing a spaceship, there's always more to discover about these amazing machines. So keep exploring, keep asking questions, and who knows? Your next big adventure might be out there among the stars! Remember, in the world of spacecraft, the sky is not the limit – it's just the beginning!

www.ingramcontent.com/pod-product-compliance
Lightning Source LLC
Chambersburg PA
CBHW071933210526
45479CB00002B/656